83rd Edition

Travel to St. Petersburg Florida

2023
People Who Know
Publishing
Jack Ross

Printed in the United States of America

This travel guide is for informational purposes only and does not constitute legal, financial, or professional advice. While every effort has been made to ensure the accuracy of the information provided, the author and publisher make no representations or warranties of any kind, express or implied, about the completeness, accuracy, reliability, suitability, or availability of the information contained in this book. The reader assumes full responsibility for any actions taken based on the information provided in this book.

People Who Know Publishing

Forward: In this book, People Who Know Publishing will provide a travel guide of 101+ things to see, do and visit in St. Petersburg Florida. We strive to make our guides as comprehensive and complete as possible. We publish travel guides on cities and countries all over the world. Feel free to check out our complete list of travel guides here:

People Who Know Publishing partners with local experts to produce travel guides on various locations. We differentiate ourselves from other travel books by focusing on areas not typically covered by others. Our guides include a detailed history of the location and its population. In addition to covering all of the "must see" areas of a location such as museums and local sights, we also provide up-to-date restaurant suggestions and local food traditions.

To make a request for a travel guide on a particular area or to join our email list to stay updated on travel tips from local experts sign up here: https://mailchi.mp/c74b62620b1f/travel-books

Be sure to confirm restaurants, addresses, and phone numbers as those may have changed since the book was published.

About the Author:

Jack Ross is a college student who was born in Westchester County, NY. He's an expert on the local "in the know" tips of the area and is an authority on Westchester and its towns. He's been featured in several publications including Business Insider and CNBC for his books.

During his spare time, he writes, plays tennis and golf and enjoys all water sports (including his latest favorite, the eFoil). Jack also enjoys traveling and is a food connoisseur throughout Westchester. Jack travels consistently and has been to majority of the states in the U.S.

Sign up for our email list to get inside access to the towns and places we cover!
>> https://mailchi.mp/c74b62620b1f/travel-books
>> https://mailchi.mp/c74b62620b1f/travel-books

Table of Contents

St. Petersburg Florida

State: Florida
Population: 261,256
Ranking in U.S.: N/A
County: Pinellas County
Founded: 1888
Tag line: N/A

Introduction

"Florida is a place of unparalleled diversity of backgrounds, experiences, and vision. It makes our culture unique, but it can also make it difficult to define a common identity and create a sense of community that reaches beyond our neighborhoods to all corners of our state." - Jeb Bush

St. Petersburg, Florida, affectionately known as "St. Pete," is a captivating coastal city that embodies the essence of the Sunshine State. Nestled along the beautiful Gulf Coast, this thriving metropolis boasts a unique combination of natural splendor, urban sophistication, and a relaxed coastal lifestyle.

At the heart of St. Petersburg's allure lies its 35 miles of pristine shoreline, including the world-renowned St. Pete Beach, Clearwater Beach, and Fort De Soto Park. The city's subtropical climate, characterized by year-round sunshine, makes it a haven for sunseekers and water enthusiasts, who flock to its shores for swimming, sunbathing, and water sports.

Beyond its sandy stretches, St. Petersburg takes pride in its flourishing arts and culture scene. The downtown area is a bustling hub of creativity, home to a diverse array of galleries, theaters, and public art installations. The Morean Arts Center and the Chihuly Collection showcase the city's commitment to fostering artistic expression, while the Mahaffey Theater and the historic Palladium Theater cater to a broad spectrum of cultural tastes.

The city's devotion to the arts culminates in the Salvador Dali Museum, which boasts the largest collection of Dali's work outside of Spain. This remarkable institution is a testament to St. Petersburg's dedication to preserving and celebrating the creative spirit.

St. Petersburg's vibrant waterfront is another of its crown jewels. Along the downtown waterfront, you'll find lush parks, bustling marinas, and a variety of open-air restaurants. Here, you can embark on scenic boat tours, indulge in fresh seafood, or simply enjoy breathtaking sunsets over the Gulf of Mexico.

St. Petersburg's commitment to fostering a sense of community is evident in its numerous festivals and events, including the annual St. Petersburg Jazz Festival, the Mainsail Arts Festival, and the St. Pete Pride Parade, among many others. These celebrations draw residents and visitors alike, showcasing the city's inclusive and welcoming spirit.

Travel to St. Petersburg Florida

As a place to call home, St. Petersburg offers an array of diverse neighborhoods, from historic districts like Old Northeast and Kenwood to vibrant downtown condominiums with stunning waterfront views. The city's diverse population is a testament to its inclusivity, with a thriving LGBTQ+ community, young professionals, families, and retirees all finding their niche.

In summary, St. Petersburg, Florida, is a city that effortlessly marries natural beauty, cultural richness, and a warm, welcoming atmosphere. Whether you're a beach lover, an art enthusiast, or someone searching for a tight-knit and diverse community, St. Petersburg provides an ideal blend of coastal living and urban vibrancy on Florida's enchanting Gulf Coast.

History

Spanish Exploration:
The first European contact with the region occurred in the early 16th century when Spanish explorers, including Ponce de León, ventured into Florida. However, it wasn't until the 19th century that significant European settlement began.

Founding of St. Petersburg:
In the late 19th century, John C. Williams, a Detroit native, and his son-in-law, Peter Demens, a Russian aristocrat, saw the potential for development in the area. They purchased land and decided to establish a town, naming it after St. Petersburg, Russia. This was done as a way to attract Russian investors for the Orange Belt Railway, which connected the area to the rest of Florida. The railroad, completed in 1888, played a crucial role in the city's early growth.

Native Inhabitants:
Long before European settlers arrived, the area that would become St. Petersburg was inhabited by the Tocobaga and Seminole Native American tribes. These indigenous communities thrived along the shores of Tampa Bay and the Pinellas Peninsula.

The Great Boom and Bust:
In the 1920s, St. Petersburg experienced a real estate and population boom, with the population doubling in just a few years. However, the collapse of the Florida land boom and the Great Depression brought hardship to the city, leading to the closure of the "Million Dollar Pier" and a decline in tourism.

St. Petersburg's natural beauty and pleasant climate made it
an attractive destination for tourists and winter residents,
earning it the nickname the "Sunshine City." Early 20th-
century visitors flocked to the city, which became known
for its waterfront parks, bathing pavilions, and the iconic
"Million Dollar Pier."

Earthquake and Rebuilding:
In 1906, the San Francisco earthquake and subsequent fires
damaged much of the city. As a result, many San Francisco
residents and businesses relocated to Oakland, accelerating
its growth. The city underwent a period of significant urban
development and expansion.

Post-World War II Growth:
After World War II, St. Petersburg experienced a
resurgence in population and tourism. The city's economy
diversified with the growth of industries such as aviation,
electronics, and tourism. Many veterans and retirees
flocked to the city, seeking the warm climate and affordable
living.

Civil Rights Movement:
St. Petersburg was not immune to the struggles of the Civil Rights Movement. Protests, sit-ins, and demonstrations occurred in the city during the 1960s, mirroring the nationwide efforts to combat racial segregation and discrimination.

Modern St. Petersburg:
St. Petersburg has continued to evolve as a vibrant and culturally rich city. It's known for its commitment to the arts, as evidenced by its museums, theaters, and galleries. The Salvador Dali Museum, in particular, draws art enthusiasts from around the world. The city's beautiful waterfront, with its parks and marinas, remains a focal point for both residents and tourists.

Contemporary St. Petersburg:
Today, St. Petersburg is a diverse, dynamic city with a thriving downtown, a burgeoning tech industry, and a strong commitment to environmental sustainability. The city's continued growth and cultural richness make it a sought-after destination for both residents and visitors.

St. Petersburg's history is a testament to its resilience and ability to adapt to changing circumstances, ultimately shaping it into the vibrant and diverse city it is today.

Economy

Tourism and Hospitality: St. Petersburg is a popular tourist destination, drawing visitors from around the world with its beautiful beaches, cultural attractions, and pleasant climate. The tourism and hospitality sector plays a significant role in the local economy, providing jobs in hotels, restaurants, and entertainment venues.

Healthcare and Medical Research: The healthcare industry is a major economic driver in St. Petersburg, with institutions like Bayfront Health St. Petersburg and Johns Hopkins All Children's Hospital. The city is also home to a growing medical research and biotechnology sector, further boosting the local economy.

Education: St. Petersburg is home to several colleges and universities, including the University of South Florida St. Petersburg and St. Petersburg College. These institutions contribute to the local economy by providing education services and research opportunities.

Maritime and Shipping: The city's proximity to Tampa Bay and the Gulf of Mexico has led to the development of a maritime industry, including shipping, marine construction, and port-related activities, which contribute to the economy.

Arts and Culture: St. Petersburg has a thriving arts and culture scene, with numerous museums, theaters, and galleries. This sector not only enriches the cultural life of the city but also generates economic activity through ticket sales, tourism, and creative industries.

Tech and Innovation: St. Petersburg has been making efforts to diversify its economy by fostering a tech and innovation ecosystem. The city is home to tech startups, co-working spaces, and organizations promoting entrepreneurship, driving economic growth in this sector.

Manufacturing: The city has a small but significant manufacturing sector, including companies involved in marine manufacturing, electronics, and aerospace components.

Transportation Systems

Roads and Highways: St. Petersburg is well-connected to the surrounding area through an extensive road network. Major highways serving the city include Interstate 275, which runs through the heart of St. Petersburg, and Interstate 175, which provides access to downtown. Several other state and local roads crisscross the city, making it accessible by car.

Public Transit: The Pinellas Suncoast Transit Authority (PSTA) operates the public transit system in St. Petersburg and the broader Pinellas County area. PSTA offers bus services that cover a wide range of routes, making it possible for residents and visitors to commute throughout the city and its suburbs. There are also trolley services in downtown St. Petersburg, providing a unique and historic mode of transportation.

Biking and Walking: St. Petersburg has been investing in becoming a more bike-friendly and pedestrian-friendly city. There are numerous bike lanes and bike-sharing programs, as well as well-maintained sidewalks, making it easy to explore the city on foot or by bicycle. The city has also introduced bike-sharing programs to encourage sustainable and healthy transportation.

Air Travel: St. Petersburg is served by several airports, including St. Pete-Clearwater International Airport (PIE) and Tampa International Airport (TPA). PIE is the closest airport and primarily serves domestic flights, while TPA offers a broader range of domestic and international connections.

Water Transportation: St. Petersburg's proximity to the Gulf of Mexico allows for water transportation options. The city has a marina and various boat ramps for recreational boating. Additionally, there are ferry services connecting St. Petersburg to nearby coastal communities.

Ridesharing and Taxi Services: Popular ridesharing services like Uber and Lyft operate in St. Petersburg, providing residents and visitors with convenient transportation options. Traditional taxi services are also available.

Tampa Bay Area Transit: St. Petersburg is part of the broader Tampa Bay area, and there are regional transportation options available. This includes the Tampa Bay Area Regional Transit Authority (TBARTA), which focuses on regional transit connectivity and planning.

Neighborhoods

Downtown St. Petersburg: The city's urban core, Downtown St. Petersburg, is a vibrant and bustling area known for its cultural attractions, dining, and nightlife. It's home to many museums, galleries, and theaters, including The Dali Museum and the Mahaffey Theater. The downtown waterfront area boasts parks, marinas, and upscale condominiums.

Old Northeast: This historic neighborhood features tree-lined streets, charming bungalows, and Mediterranean Revival homes. Old Northeast is a favorite among residents for its walkability, proximity to downtown, and its picturesque beauty.

Kenwood: Known for its artsy and eclectic vibe, Kenwood is a historic district filled with colorful bungalows and craftsman-style homes. It has a strong arts community and hosts the popular "Kenwood Artists' Enclave" events.

Historic Roser Park: One of the city's oldest neighborhoods, Roser Park, is known for its historic architecture, including Spanish Revival, Mediterranean, and Craftsman-style homes. The neighborhood is located near downtown and features a scenic park.

Uptown: Uptown St. Petersburg is an up-and-coming area known for its mix of historic homes and modern developments. It's also home to the 22nd Street South Business District, which is experiencing revitalization efforts.

Food

Seafood: Given its coastal location, St. Petersburg is renowned for its fresh seafood. You can savor Gulf of Mexico catches, including grouper, snapper, shrimp, and oysters. Try a classic dish like "Grouper Sandwich" or "Shrimp and Grits" at local seafood restaurants.

Cuban Cuisine: St. Petersburg has a strong Cuban influence, and you can find authentic Cuban dishes like "Ropa Vieja" (shredded beef), "Cuban Sandwiches," and "Picadillo" at Cuban eateries throughout the city.

Florida Key Lime Pie: A quintessential Florida dessert, Key Lime Pie is a must-try. The dessert features a tangy and sweet filling made from Key limes and is often served with a graham cracker crust.

Southern Comfort Food: You can find classic Southern comfort dishes like "Fried Chicken," "Biscuits and Gravy," and "Collard Greens" in St. Petersburg's restaurants. These dishes offer a taste of traditional Southern cuisine.

Fresh Tropical Fruits: St. Petersburg's climate allows for the growth of various tropical fruits, including mangoes, papayas, and guava. Enjoy these fruits in various forms, such as fresh fruit salads, smoothies, or desserts.

Craft Beer and Breweries: St. Petersburg has a thriving craft beer scene with numerous local breweries. Sample a variety of craft beers, from IPAs to stouts, and enjoy the city's craft beer culture.

Farm-to-Table Fare: St. Petersburg embraces the farm-to-table movement, and you can find restaurants that focus on fresh, locally sourced ingredients in their dishes. These restaurants often offer seasonal menus with an emphasis on sustainability.

Here are our ten favorite restaurant recommendations!

1.The Mill Restaurant: Known for its innovative Southern cuisine, The Mill offers a farm-to-table dining experience. The menu features dishes like Fried Green Tomatoes, Shrimp and Grits, and Bacon-Wrapped Meatloaf.

2.Il Ritorno: A highly-rated Italian restaurant, Il Ritorno offers a contemporary take on classic Italian dishes. The menu includes house-made pasta, wood-fired pizza, and a selection of small plates.

3.Z Grille: This restaurant specializes in American and Gulf Coast cuisine. Dishes include Cedar Plank Salmon, BBQ Pork Belly Tacos, and inventive burgers. It's known for its use of locally-sourced ingredients.

4.Birch & Vine: Located in the historic Birchwood Hotel, this restaurant offers modern American cuisine with a farm-to-table focus. The rooftop bar and picturesque views add to the dining experience.

5.The Library: Social Eatery and Drinkery: A cozy and inviting spot, The Library serves a diverse menu with options like Lamb Chops, Crispy Duck Confit, and a variety of craft cocktails.

6.Noble Crust: Specializing in Southern-inspired Italian cuisine, Noble Crust offers dishes such as Shrimp and Grits, Wood-Grilled Pizzas, and creative cocktails.

Travel to St. Petersburg Florida

7.*Locale Market: A gourmet food hall with various dining options, Locale Market allows you to explore a range of cuisines. It features a raw bar, sushi, pizza, and more, and it's a great place for food enthusiasts.*

8.*Red Mesa Cantina: A popular spot for Mexican cuisine, Red Mesa Cantina offers a diverse menu with options like Tacos al Pastor, Enchiladas, and a selection of tequilas and margaritas.*

9.*Rococo Steak: Known for its upscale steakhouse experience, Rococo Steak serves high-quality cuts of meat, fresh seafood, and an extensive wine list.*

10.*Munch's Sundries: A beloved local diner, Munch's is famous for its hearty breakfasts, comfort food, and friendly atmosphere. The "Hubcap Burger" is a must-try.*

Travel to St. Petersburg Florida

Nightlife

The Ale and the Witch: This craft beer and live music venue in downtown St. Petersburg is known for its extensive selection of craft beers and a relaxed atmosphere. Live bands often perform on the outdoor stage, making it a popular spot for music enthusiasts.

Ruby's Elixir: Located on Central Avenue, Ruby's Elixir is a jazz and blues club that hosts live music acts. The intimate setting and well-crafted cocktails make it a favorite for those seeking a sophisticated night out.

Five Bucks Drinkery: A popular downtown spot, Five Bucks offers affordable drinks and a fun, laid-back atmosphere. It's a great place to socialize with friends, play pool, or enjoy live DJ sets.

Jannus Live: This outdoor concert venue in the heart of St. Petersburg hosts a variety of musical performances, from indie bands to well-known artists. It's a fantastic spot for live music and outdoor entertainment.

The Bends: A hip dive bar with a great selection of craft beers and cocktails. It's known for its indie music playlist, retro video games, and a friendly, unpretentious atmosphere.

Enigma St. Pete: A popular LGBTQ+ nightclub, Enigma features drag shows, dancing, and themed events. It's a lively and inclusive place to enjoy the nightlife.

Local Traditions & Customs

Supporting Local Sports Teams: St. Petersburg residents are passionate about their sports, particularly baseball. The Tampa Bay Rays, a Major League Baseball team, play their home games at Tropicana Field in St. Petersburg. Attending baseball games and showing support for the Rays is a local tradition, especially during the baseball season.

Beach Lifestyle: St. Petersburg's beautiful beaches, including St. Pete Beach, Treasure Island, and Fort De Soto Park, play a central role in the local culture. It's customary for residents to spend weekends or evenings enjoying the beach, whether for swimming, sunbathing, or taking part in water sports and outdoor activities.

Art and Culture: The city's commitment to arts and culture is a cherished tradition. Residents often attend art festivals, music performances, and theatrical productions. Events like the St. Petersburg Jazz Festival and the Mainsail Arts Festival have become annual traditions that celebrate the city's artistic spirit.

Local Markets: St. Petersburg hosts numerous farmers' markets and craft fairs throughout the year. It's a tradition for residents to visit these markets to buy fresh, locally grown produce, artisanal products, and handmade crafts.

St. Pete Pride: St. Petersburg is known for its vibrant LGBTQ+ community, and the annual St. Pete Pride Parade and Festival is a significant event that celebrates diversity, inclusion, and equal rights. This colorful and lively event attracts both locals and visitors.

What to buy?

Beachwear and Souvenirs: Given the city's stunning beaches, you'll find a wide array of beachwear, including swimwear, flip-flops, and sun hats. You can also find an assortment of beach-themed souvenirs, such as T-shirts, beach towels, and seashell crafts.

Art and Local Crafts: St. Petersburg is known for its vibrant arts scene, so consider purchasing local art and crafts as souvenirs. Look for unique pieces at local galleries and craft markets, including paintings, sculptures, jewelry, and pottery.

Craft Beer and Local Spirits: Florida's craft beer scene is thriving, and you can explore a variety of local breweries in St. Petersburg. Purchase a few bottles or cans of craft beer or local spirits to enjoy or take home as gifts.

Jewelry: St. Petersburg offers a range of artisan jewelry made by local designers. Look for pieces that incorporate beachy elements like sea glass or shells.

Key Lime Products: Key lime is a quintessential Florida flavor, and you can find a variety of key lime products, including key lime pie, key lime cookies, key lime sauces, and key lime-scented bath and body products.

Tropical Plants: If you have a green thumb or are looking for a unique and lasting souvenir, consider purchasing a tropical plant like a potted palm, orchid, or succulent that can thrive indoors.

Finally, here are the five most famous people from the city!

1.Al Lang (1888-1960): Al Lang was a prominent sports figure and the mayor of St. Petersburg from 1949 to 1960. He is best known for his efforts to bring Major League Baseball spring training to the city, leading to St. Petersburg becoming a spring training hub and the home of the Tampa Bay Rays.

2.Elizabeth Eckford: While not originally from St. Petersburg, Elizabeth Eckford became a notable figure in the Civil Rights Movement. She was one of the "Little Rock Nine" who desegregated Little Rock Central High School in 1957 and later moved to St. Petersburg, where she continued her civil rights activism.

3.Dali Lama XIV: The 14th Dalai Lama, Tenzin Gyatso, visited St. Petersburg in 2003, and his presence in the city left a lasting impact. He is a prominent spiritual leader and Nobel Peace Prize laureate known for his teachings on compassion and peace.

4.Lorraine Hansberry (1930-1965): The playwright and author Lorraine Hansberry, best known for her groundbreaking play "A Raisin in the Sun," spent some of her formative years in St. Petersburg. Her work continues to be influential in American literature and theater.

5.Janet Petro: Janet Petro is a former astronaut who was born in St. Petersburg. She joined NASA in 1998 and served as a mission specialist for Space Shuttle missions. Her contributions to space exploration and research have made her a notable figure in the field.

101+ things to do in the city

1. Visit the Salvador Dali Museum.
2. Explore the Museum of Fine Arts.
3. Enjoy the Florida Holocaust Museum.
4. Take a stroll through Sunken Gardens.
5. Go to the Morean Arts Center.
6. Discover the Chihuly Collection.
7. Attend a performance at the Mahaffey Theater.
8. Explore the Imagine Museum.
9. Visit the Dr. Carter G. Woodson African American Museum.
10. Take a walk through the St. Petersburg Museum of History.
11. Experience live theater at American Stage Theatre.
12. Enjoy a show at the Palladium Theater.
13. Attend the St. Petersburg Shakespeare Festival.
14. Take a guided mural tour.
15. Discover the Duncan McClellan Gallery.
16. Visit Great Explorations Children's Museum.
17. Explore the Suncoast Seabird Sanctuary.
18. Enjoy the Boyd Hill Nature Preserve.
19. Go birdwatching at Fort De Soto Park.
20. Visit Weedon Island Preserve.
21. Explore Sawgrass Lake Park.
22. Go hiking at Brooker Creek Preserve.
23. Enjoy the Suncoast Primate Sanctuary.
24. Visit Heritage Village.
25. Explore the Florida Botanical Gardens.
26. Discover the Largo Central Park Nature Preserve.
27. Attend a Tampa Bay Rowdies soccer game.
28. Catch a Tampa Bay Rays baseball game.
29. Explore Tropicana Field.
30. Visit Al Lang Stadium for soccer games and events.
31. Enjoy a round of golf at local courses.
32. Try stand-up paddleboarding on the Gulf.
33. Go fishing off the St. Petersburg Pier.
34. Experience the annual Firestone Grand Prix.
35. Join a guided kayaking tour.
36. Explore local beaches: St. Pete Beach, Pass-a-Grille Beach, Treasure Island
37. Relax on the pristine Fort De Soto Beach.
38. Go shelling at Shell Key Preserve.
39. Experience parasailing on the Gulf of Mexico.
40. Take a dolphin-watching tour.

41. Enjoy sunset cruises.
42. Try jet skiing or wave-running.
43. Take a scenic boat tour of the area.
44. Go deep-sea fishing in the Gulf.
45. Explore the vibrant downtown waterfront.
46. Enjoy a day at North Straub Park.
47. Visit Vinoy Park for picnics and events.
48. Relax in South Straub Park.
49. Go to Flora Wylie Park for its playground.
50. Discover the nature trails of Coquina Key Park.
51. Enjoy a game of beach volleyball.
52. Take a morning yoga class on the beach.
53. Play frisbee at a beach park.
54. Explore Maximo Park and its trails.
55. Visit Crescent Lake Park.
56. Attend one of the city's frequent festivals.
57. Take part in the annual St. Pete Pride Parade.
58. Explore the Saturday Morning Market.
59. Attend the Mainsail Arts Festival.
60. Enjoy Localtopia, a celebration of local businesses.
61. Experience the SunLit Festival.
62. Visit the St. Petersburg International Folk Fair.
63. Attend the St. Pete Seafood and Music Festival.
64. Explore the St. Petersburg Power & Sailboat Show.
65. Participate in the Tampa Bay Blues Festival.
66. Go to the St. Pete Beach Corey Area Craft Festival.
67. Attend the Firestone Grand Prix.
68. Discover the St. Pete Wine & Food Festival.
69. Visit the annual Ribfest food and music festival.
70. Enjoy the SHINE Mural Festival.
71. Visit the Saturday Artwalk in the Warehouse Arts District.
72. Experience the SHINE Mural Festival.
73. Explore the Gandy Bridge Trail.
74. Bike the Pinellas Trail.
75. Walk or run along the Legacy Trail.
76. Hike at Boca Ciega Millennium Park.
77. Visit the Florida Orange Groves Winery.
78. Enjoy a brewery tour at local craft breweries.
79. Take a coffee shop tour in downtown St. Petersburg.
80. Explore the Dade Battlefield Historic State Park.
81. Discover the Lake Maggiore Environmental Education Center.
82. Visit the St. Petersburg Shuffleboard Club.

83.Attend the St. Pete Beach Classic.

84 Join a community beach cleanup event.

85. Take a historic preservation tour.

86.Enjoy a round of mini-golf.

87.Visit the Sunken Gardens for a yoga class.

88.Explore the Grand Central District for shopping.

89.Attend the St. Petersburg Second Saturday ArtWalk.

90.Take a Segway tour of the city.

91.Experience a dolphin encounter program at the Clearwater Marine Aquarium.

92.Visit Tampa Bay Watch Discovery Center.

93.Explore Tampa Bay's islands by ferry.

94.Take a scenic drive along the Gulf of Mexico.

95.Discover the history of St. Petersburg through local historic districts.

96.Attend the St. Pete Folk Fair.

97.Explore local vintage shops and boutiques.

98.Discover the city's diverse culinary scene.

99.Experience St. Petersburg's nightlife at bars and clubs.

100.Join a craft beer tour to sample local brews.

101.Go wine tasting at local wineries.

102.Enjoy a rooftop dinner with a view.

103.Attend a waterfront festival at Vinoy Park.

104.Explore the history of Sunken Gardens.

105.Take a historic walking tour.

106.Attend a live music event at a local venue.

107.Visit a local farmers' market.

108.Go thrift shopping in the city's thrift stores.

109.Join a community gardening project.

110.Take a scenic drive through local parks.

1. Visit the Salvador Dali Museum.

Visiting the Salvador Dali Museum is a must-do activity when you're in St. Petersburg, Florida. Here's what you can expect when you visit this renowned museum:

Explore Dali's Masterpieces: The Salvador Dali Museum houses one of the most comprehensive collections of works by the famous Surrealist artist, Salvador Dali. You'll have the opportunity to see some of his most iconic and thought-provoking paintings, sculptures, and drawings.

Admire the Architecture: The museum's building itself is a work of art. Designed by architect Yann Weymouth, the structure is a masterpiece that complements Dali's artistic style. The striking geodesic glass structure, known as the "Enigma," is an architectural wonder.

Experience Surrealism: Dali was a pioneer of the Surrealist movement, and his works often challenge conventional reality. As you explore the museum, you'll encounter mind-bending and dreamlike images that will provoke your imagination.

Educational Programs: The museum offers educational programs, guided tours, and interactive exhibits that provide insight into Dali's life, art, and the Surrealist movement. You can gain a deeper understanding of the artist's creative process and influences.

Temporary Exhibitions: In addition to the permanent collection, the museum hosts temporary exhibitions featuring the works of Dali's contemporaries and other artists, adding to the cultural richness of your visit.

Museum Store: The museum's gift shop offers a wide range of Dali-inspired merchandise, including books, prints, clothing, and unique gifts. It's a great place to pick up souvenirs.

Gardens: The museum features a beautifully landscaped garden with a labyrinth and a wishing tree. It's a tranquil space where you can relax and reflect on your visit.

Café Gala: Named after Dali's wife, Café Gala is the museum's on-site café where you can enjoy Spanish-inspired cuisine, coffee, and desserts. The café's outdoor seating is particularly pleasant.

Events and Workshops: The museum frequently hosts special events, workshops, and lectures that provide opportunities to engage with the art and learn more about Dali's life and works.

Photography: Photography is allowed in most areas of the museum, so you can capture memories of your visit. Just be sure to follow the museum's photography guidelines.

Visiting the Salvador Dali Museum is an enriching and thought-provoking experience for art enthusiasts, history buffs, and anyone looking to explore the world of Surrealism. Don't forget to check the museum's operating hours and any special exhibitions that may be taking place during your visit.

2.Explore the Museum of Fine Arts.

Exploring the Museum of Fine Arts in St. Petersburg, Florida, is a delightful and culturally enriching experience. Here's what you can expect when you visit this distinguished museum:

Art Collections: The Museum of Fine Arts houses an extensive and diverse collection of art spanning various periods and styles. You can admire works of art from ancient to contemporary, including paintings, sculptures, decorative arts, and more.

European and American Art: The museum's collection features European and American paintings from renowned artists. You can view masterpieces by artists such as Monet, Cézanne, O'Keeffe, and many others.

Asian Art: Explore the Asian art collection, which includes an impressive array of Chinese, Japanese, and Korean artworks, ceramics, and textiles. The Asian collection offers a glimpse into the rich cultural heritage of the East.

Decorative Arts: The museum boasts a fine collection of decorative arts, including exquisite glassware, pottery, and porcelain from various time periods and regions. These items showcase the craftsmanship and artistic excellence of their respective eras.

Ancient Art: Admire ancient art and artifacts from civilizations such as Greece, Rome, and Egypt. The museum's collection includes pottery, sculptures, and other pieces that provide insight into the art and history of these cultures.

Special Exhibitions: In addition to its permanent collection, the museum hosts temporary exhibitions that feature a wide range of artists, themes, and styles. These exhibitions add to the diversity of your visit and may introduce you to new and exciting works of art.

Educational Programs: The museum offers educational programs, guided tours, and interactive exhibits that provide context and insight into the artworks. These programs can enhance your understanding and appreciation of the art on display.

Museum Store: The museum's gift shop offers art-related books, prints, jewelry, and unique gifts. It's a great place to find souvenirs or gifts for art lovers.

Courtyard and Gardens: The museum features a peaceful courtyard and gardens where you can relax and enjoy the serene surroundings. It's an ideal spot to take a break during your visit.

Café: The museum's café offers a selection of light refreshments, including coffee, pastries, and snacks. It's a convenient place to refuel and rest.

Events and Workshops: Keep an eye on the museum's events calendar for lectures, workshops, and special events that provide additional opportunities to engage with the art and its cultural significance.

Visiting the Museum of Fine Arts in St. Petersburg allows you to immerse yourself in a world of art, culture, and history. It's a great destination for art enthusiasts, history buffs, and anyone who appreciates the beauty and creativity of human expression. Be sure to check the museum's operating hours and any special exhibitions that may be on display during your visit.

3.Enjoy the Florida Holocaust Museum.

Exploring the Florida Holocaust Museum in St. Petersburg is a powerful and educational experience. Here's what you can expect when you visit this museum:

Holocaust History: The museum is dedicated to preserving and sharing the history of the Holocaust. You will find a wealth of information about this tragic period, including the events leading up to the Holocaust, the experiences of survivors, and the consequences of the genocide.

Exhibits: The museum features a range of permanent and temporary exhibits that delve into the history and personal stories of those affected by the Holocaust. These exhibits often include photographs, artifacts, documents, and interactive displays.

Artifacts: You can see authentic artifacts from the Holocaust, such as clothing, personal items, and items related to life in concentration camps. These artifacts provide a tangible connection to the past.

Survivor Testimonies: The museum often includes survivor testimonies and oral histories in its exhibits. These personal accounts provide a moving and firsthand perspective on the Holocaust.

Educational Programs: The museum offers educational programs for visitors of all ages. You can participate in guided tours, lectures, and workshops to gain a deeper understanding of the Holocaust's historical and moral lessons.

Tolerance and Human Rights: The museum places a strong emphasis on the importance of tolerance, human rights, and the prevention of future genocides. Visitors are encouraged to reflect on these themes.

Remembering the Victims: The museum serves as a place of remembrance for the millions of victims who suffered and perished during the Holocaust. The memorial aspect of the museum allows for quiet reflection.

Community Engagement: The Florida Holocaust Museum is involved in various community outreach programs and events, promoting education and awareness about the Holocaust and its lessons.

Art and Culture: The museum occasionally hosts art and cultural exhibitions related to the Holocaust and human rights issues, providing a broader perspective on the subject.

Gift Shop: The museum's gift shop offers books, educational materials, and commemorative items related to the Holocaust. Purchases support the museum's mission.

Visiting the Florida Holocaust Museum is a somber but important experience that offers insights into a dark period of history. It serves as a reminder of the consequences of hatred and the importance of tolerance and human rights. As you explore the museum, you'll have the opportunity to reflect on the lessons of the Holocaust and its relevance to contemporary issues. Be sure to check the museum's operating hours and any special exhibits or events that may be taking place during your visit.

4. Take a stroll through Sunken Gardens.

Taking a stroll through Sunken Gardens in St. Petersburg, Florida, is a wonderful way to enjoy the beauty of nature and experience a tranquil oasis. Here's what you can expect when you visit this lush and historic garden:

Botanical Paradise: Sunken Gardens is a 100-year-old living museum featuring a diverse collection of tropical plants, exotic flora, and vibrant flowers. You'll be immersed in a lush, green paradise as you explore the gardens.

Walking Paths: The gardens offer winding paths and walkways that lead you through the various sections of the garden. You can leisurely explore the different plant species and themed garden areas.

Floral Displays: Enjoy the stunning displays of colorful and fragrant flowers throughout the gardens. Different seasons bring different blooms, so the garden is ever-changing and provides a visual feast for nature enthusiasts and photographers.

Koi Ponds: Sunken Gardens is home to numerous koi ponds with beautiful, brightly colored fish. You can watch the graceful fish swim and enjoy the serenity of the water features.

Waterfalls: The gardens feature small waterfalls and cascades, adding to the overall ambiance of relaxation and tranquility.

Bamboo Garden: Explore the enchanting Bamboo Garden, which features various bamboo species, creating a peaceful and shaded environment.

Flamingos: Sunken Gardens is known for its resident flock of Chilean flamingos. These elegant birds are a delight to watch and photograph.

Wedding Venue: The gardens are a popular venue for weddings and special events. The picturesque setting provides a romantic backdrop for ceremonies and celebrations.

Educational Programs: Sunken Gardens offers educational programs, including horticultural classes and guided tours. You can learn more about the plant species and the history of the gardens.

Photography: The gardens are a favorite spot for photographers, both amateur and professional. The natural beauty and vibrant colors make it a prime location for capturing memorable shots.

Gift Shop: The gardens have a gift shop where you can purchase plants, gardening accessories, and unique botanical gifts.

Events: Sunken Gardens occasionally hosts special events and workshops, so check the garden's calendar for any upcoming activities during your visit.

Visiting Sunken Gardens provides a peaceful and rejuvenating experience, making it an ideal destination for nature lovers, garden enthusiasts, and anyone looking to escape into a tropical paradise within the heart of the city. Be sure to check the garden's operating hours and any special events or classes that may be taking place during your visit.

5.Go to the Morean Arts Center.

Visiting the Morean Arts Center in St. Petersburg, Florida, offers a captivating artistic experience. Here's what you can expect when you explore this cultural institution:

Art Exhibitions: The Morean Arts Center features a diverse range of contemporary art exhibitions, showcasing the works of local, national, and international artists. You can explore various art forms, from painting and sculpture to photography and multimedia installations.

Permanent Collection: The center has a permanent collection of artworks that highlights the artistic talent and creative expression of the local community. It's a great opportunity to discover the art scene in St. Petersburg.

Glass Studio and Hot Shop: The Morean Arts Center is known for its glassblowing studio and hot shop, where you can watch artists create stunning glass pieces. Demonstrations and workshops are often offered to provide a hands-on experience.

Travel to St. Petersburg Florida

Art Classes and Workshops: The center offers art classes and workshops for all ages and skill levels. You can participate in classes ranging from painting and pottery to photography and digital media.

Family-Friendly Programs: The Morean Arts Center provides family-friendly programs and events, making it a great place for children and families to engage with art and creativity.

Art Shop: The center has an art shop where you can purchase unique, handcrafted items, including jewelry, ceramics, glassware, and paintings. It's a fantastic place to find one-of-a-kind gifts and keepsakes.

Events and Openings: The Morean Arts Center hosts art openings and special events, providing opportunities to meet artists, curators, and fellow art enthusiasts.

Educational Opportunities: If you're interested in art education, the center offers classes, lectures, and opportunities to learn about various art techniques and styles.

Community Involvement: The Morean Arts Center is actively engaged with the local community, and it often participates in community events and collaborations.

Historic Building: The center is housed in a historic building that adds to the overall ambiance and charm of the visit. The architecture itself is an interesting element to explore.

Artistic Inspiration: Whether you're an artist or an art appreciator, a visit to the Morean Arts Center can provide inspiration and insight into the contemporary art scene in St. Petersburg.

Local Artists: The center often showcases the work of local artists, giving you the opportunity to support and connect with the creative talents in the area.

Visiting the Morean Arts Center is an enriching and culturally stimulating experience, offering a chance to engage with contemporary art, explore various forms of creative expression, and even try your hand at making art. Be sure to check the center's operating hours, current exhibitions, and any upcoming events or classes that may coincide with your visit.

6.Discover the Chihuly Collection.

Exploring the Chihuly Collection in St. Petersburg, Florida, is an extraordinary artistic experience. Here's what you can expect when you visit this collection:

Dale Chihuly's Glass Art: The Chihuly Collection is dedicated to the works of internationally acclaimed glass artist Dale Chihuly. You'll have the opportunity to view a stunning array of his glass sculptures, installations, and blown glass creations.

Unique Glassworks: Chihuly's art is renowned for its vibrant colors, intricate designs, and innovative use of glass. The collection features a wide range of his works, each one showcasing the artist's creativity and mastery of the medium.

Indoor and Outdoor Displays: The collection is housed both indoors and outdoors, with pieces exhibited in a gallery setting as well as in the lush gardens surrounding the museum. You can enjoy the interplay between Chihuly's glass art and the natural world.

Diverse Art Forms: Chihuly's art encompasses various forms, including sculptures, chandeliers, installations, and large-scale glassworks. The collection provides a comprehensive look at his artistic evolution and versatility.

Guided Tours: Guided tours are available to provide in-depth insights into Chihuly's life and art. Knowledgeable guides share stories and details about the artist's creative process and the significance of each piece.

Art Shop: The collection's gift shop offers Chihuly-inspired merchandise, including glass art, prints, books, and unique gifts. It's a great place to find artistic souvenirs.

Educational Programs: The museum provides educational programs and workshops for visitors of all ages. You can learn about the techniques and inspiration behind Chihuly's glass art.

Events and Exhibitions: The Chihuly Collection occasionally hosts special exhibitions and events, so be sure to check for any ongoing or upcoming activities during your visit.

Photography: Photography is allowed in many areas of the collection, so you can capture the beauty of Chihuly's glass art and the enchanting surroundings.

Local Art Scene: Visiting the Chihuly Collection offers an opportunity to connect with St. Petersburg's vibrant art scene and explore the impact of a world-renowned artist on the local cultural landscape.

Artistic Inspiration: Whether you're an artist or an art enthusiast, the Chihuly Collection can inspire creativity and appreciation for the artistic possibilities of glass.

Museum Setting: The collection is housed in a contemporary and architecturally interesting building, providing an engaging environment for viewing Chihuly's art.

Visiting the Chihuly Collection is a visually captivating and inspiring experience, allowing you to immerse yourself in the mesmerizing world of Dale Chihuly's glass art. Be sure to check the collection's operating hours and any special exhibitions or events that may be taking place during your visit.

7.Attend a performance at the Mahaffey Theater.

Attending a performance at the Mahaffey Theater in St. Petersburg, Florida, is a cultural delight. Here's what you can expect when you experience a show at this renowned venue:

Diverse Performances: The Mahaffey Theater hosts a wide range of performances, including Broadway musicals, classical concerts, comedy shows, dance performances, and live music acts. You can choose from an array of entertainment options.

Elegant Venue: The theater is known for its elegant and comfortable interior, providing an enjoyable and immersive setting for performances. The acoustics are exceptional, ensuring that you have a quality audio-visual experience.

Broadway Shows: The Mahaffey often hosts touring Broadway productions, allowing you to enjoy popular and critically acclaimed musicals and plays right in St. Petersburg.

Live Music: You can catch live music performances spanning various genres, from classical and orchestral to rock, pop, jazz, and more. Renowned musicians and bands often grace the stage.

Comedy Acts: Many well-known comedians perform stand-up comedy at the theater, providing evenings of laughter and entertainment.

Dance Performances: Enjoy the artistry of professional dance companies, from ballet to contemporary dance, in spectacular live productions.

Symphony and Orchestra: The Florida Orchestra frequently performs at the Mahaffey Theater, offering a chance to enjoy classical music and symphonic concerts.

Family-Friendly Shows: The theater hosts family-friendly performances, making it an ideal destination for parents and children to enjoy live entertainment together.

Special Events: Keep an eye out for special events and holiday performances, as the theater often hosts shows to celebrate various occasions and seasons.

Lobby and Intermission: The theater's lobby and facilities provide an excellent space to relax during intermissions, socialize, and enjoy refreshments.

Art Gallery: The Mahaffey Theater often features an art gallery, showcasing the work of local artists and adding to the cultural experience.

Café and Dining: The theater has a café and dining options, allowing you to enjoy a meal or drinks before or after the performance.

Accessible Location: The Mahaffey Theater is conveniently located in downtown St. Petersburg, making it easily accessible with nearby parking options.

Community Engagement: The theater frequently engages with the local community by hosting educational programs, outreach events, and collaborations with local arts organizations.

Check the Schedule: Be sure to check the theater's schedule for upcoming performances and purchase tickets in advance to secure your seats for the show you want to attend.

Attending a performance at the Mahaffey Theater is a cultural highlight in St. Petersburg, providing you with an opportunity to enjoy world-class entertainment in a sophisticated and welcoming atmosphere. Be sure to check the theater's website for show schedules, ticket information, and any additional details about the performance you wish to see.

8.Explore the Imagine Museum.

Exploring the Imagine Museum in St. Petersburg, Florida, is a captivating experience that allows you to immerse yourself in the world of contemporary glass art. Here's what you can expect when you visit this unique museum:

Glass Art Collections: The Imagine Museum is dedicated to contemporary glass art. You'll have the opportunity to view a diverse and impressive collection of glass sculptures and artworks created by renowned artists from around the world.

Innovative Glass Techniques: The museum showcases a wide range of glass techniques and styles, including blown glass, kiln-formed glass, flameworked glass, and cast glass. You'll witness the innovative and creative approaches these artists use to work with glass as a medium.

Permanent and Rotating Exhibits: The museum features both permanent and rotating exhibitions, providing a fresh and dynamic experience with each visit. These exhibits often explore various themes and artistic expressions.

Educational Programs: The Imagine Museum offers educational programs, including guided tours, glassblowing demonstrations, and glass art workshops. These programs provide insight into the art form and its creative process.

Glassblowing Demonstrations: The museum often hosts live glassblowing demonstrations, allowing you to witness the mesmerizing process of shaping molten glass into intricate forms.

Interactive Displays: Some exhibits feature interactive displays that engage visitors in the art-making process, offering hands-on experiences to create their own glass art.

Photography: Photography is typically allowed in many areas of the museum, so you can capture the beauty of the glass art and your experience.

Art Shop: The museum's gift shop offers glass art pieces, jewelry, books, and unique glass-related gifts. It's an excellent place to find artistic souvenirs.

Artistic Inspiration: A visit to the Imagine Museum can be an inspirational experience, exposing you to the limitless possibilities of glass as an artistic medium.

Community Engagement: The museum is actively involved in the local community, collaborating with artists, schools, and organizations to promote glass art and creative expression.

Events and Workshops: Check the museum's calendar for special events, workshops, and lectures that provide additional opportunities to engage with glass art.

Architectural Beauty: The building that houses the museum is architecturally interesting, providing an aesthetically pleasing backdrop for the art within.

Visiting the Imagine Museum offers a unique and visually stunning experience, allowing you to appreciate the artistry and creativity of glass as a medium for contemporary artistic expression. Be sure to check the museum's operating hours, current exhibitions, and any special events or programs that may be taking place during your visit.

9. Visit the Dr. Carter G. Woodson African American Museum.

Visiting the Dr. Carter G. Woodson African American Museum in St. Petersburg, Florida, is an opportunity to explore African American history, culture, and contributions. Here's what you can expect when you visit this important museum:

African American History: The museum is dedicated to preserving, showcasing, and celebrating the history and culture of African Americans, with a particular focus on the local and regional context.

Exhibitions: The Dr. Carter G. Woodson African American Museum features a variety of exhibitions that highlight the achievements, struggles, and stories of African Americans. These exhibits often cover a wide range of topics, from civil rights to the arts and sciences.

Travel to St. Petersburg Florida

Permanent and Rotating Exhibits: The museum has both permanent exhibits that provide a foundational understanding of African American history and rotating exhibits that explore different aspects of the culture and heritage.

Carter G. Woodson: Learn about the life and work of Dr. Carter G. Woodson, the renowned African American historian, educator, and founder of Black History Month. The museum is named in his honor.

Local History: The museum provides insight into the African American history of St. Petersburg and the Tampa Bay region, offering a deeper understanding of the local community's contributions and challenges.

Educational Programs: The museum offers educational programs, lectures, and workshops that promote a greater understanding of African American history and culture. These programs are often engaging and informative.

Community Engagement: The Dr. Carter G. Woodson African American Museum actively engages with the local community through events, partnerships, and collaborations with schools and organizations.

Art and Culture: Explore the artistic and cultural achievements of African Americans through various art forms, including visual art, music, literature, and performing arts.

Special Events: Check the museum's calendar for special events, celebrations, and lectures that may coincide with your visit. These events often provide opportunities to interact with the community and learn more about African American culture.

Gift Shop: The museum's gift shop offers a selection of books, art, and cultural items related to African American heritage. It's a great place to find educational materials and gifts.

Visiting the Dr. Carter G. Woodson African American Museum is an enriching and enlightening experience, allowing you to deepen your knowledge of African American history and culture. It's an important destination for individuals interested in American history, social justice, and cultural diversity. Be sure to check the museum's operating hours and any special exhibitions or events that may be taking place during your visit.

10. Take a walk through the St. Petersburg Museum of History.

Taking a walk through the St. Petersburg Museum of History is a journey through the rich and diverse history of the city and its surrounding region. Here's what you can expect when you explore this historical museum:

Local History: The museum is dedicated to preserving and presenting the history of St. Petersburg, Florida, and the Tampa Bay region. You'll gain insights into the city's evolution from its early days to the present.

Permanent Exhibits: The museum features permanent exhibits that cover a wide range of historical topics, including the city's founding, early settlements, industries, and notable figures who have shaped St. Petersburg's history.

Local Artifacts: You can view a diverse collection of artifacts, photographs, and documents that provide a tangible connection to the past. These items help illustrate the region's history and cultural heritage.

Special Exhibitions: The museum often hosts special exhibitions that delve into specific aspects of local history, offering fresh and dynamic content for repeat visitors.

Native American History: Learn about the Native American communities that inhabited the Tampa Bay area and their contributions to the region's history.

Early Explorers and Settlers: Explore the journeys of early explorers, pioneers, and settlers who ventured into the region, and the challenges they faced.

Maritime Heritage: Discover the maritime history of St. Petersburg, including its role as a fishing and boating hub.

Sports and Culture: The museum highlights the city's contributions to sports and culture, including its role in baseball history and its vibrant arts community.

Educational Programs: The St. Petersburg Museum of History offers educational programs, lectures, and workshops for visitors of all ages, making it an excellent destination for learning about local history.

Interactive Displays: Some exhibits feature interactive displays, allowing visitors to engage with the history in a hands-on manner.

Community Engagement: The museum actively engages with the local community, collaborating with schools, organizations, and cultural institutions to promote historical awareness and education.

Gift Shop: The museum's gift shop offers a selection of history-related books, memorabilia, and unique gifts. It's a great place to find souvenirs or educational materials.

Visiting the St. Petersburg Museum of History provides a deeper understanding of the city's heritage and the people and events that have shaped its identity. Whether you're a history enthusiast or simply curious about the local past, the museum offers a fascinating and educational experience. Be sure to check the museum's operating hours, special exhibitions, and any upcoming events that may enhance your visit.

11.Experience live theater at American Stage Theatre.

Experiencing live theater at American Stage Theatre in St. Petersburg, Florida, is a cultural and artistic delight. Here's what you can expect when you attend a performance at this renowned theater:

Diverse Productions: American Stage Theatre offers a wide range of theatrical productions, including classic and contemporary plays, musicals, dramas, comedies, and thought-provoking works.

Talented Cast and Crew: The theater features talented actors, directors, and production teams dedicated to delivering high-quality performances. You can expect captivating and immersive shows.

Intimate Venue: American Stage Theatre provides an intimate setting, allowing you to feel close to the action on stage and fully engage with the performances.

Varied Genres: The theater showcases an array of theatrical genres, ensuring that there's something for everyone, from Shakespearean classics to modern, cutting-edge productions.

Educational Programs: American Stage Theatre offers educational programs and opportunities for aspiring actors, playwrights, and those interested in theater arts. You can participate in workshops and classes to enhance your understanding of theater.

Special Events: Check the theater's calendar for special events, such as opening nights, post-show discussions, and behind-the-scenes tours. These events provide insight into the creative process and opportunities to interact with the cast and crew.

Community Engagement: The theater actively engages with the local community through outreach programs, partnerships with schools, and initiatives that promote the arts and cultural enrichment.

Lobby and Intermission: The theater's lobby and facilities offer a comfortable space to mingle with fellow theatergoers during intermissions and before and after the performance.

Artistic Inspiration: Attending live theater at American Stage Theatre can be an inspiring experience, whether you're an actor, director, or simply an appreciator of the arts.

Access to the Arts: The theater contributes to the cultural vibrancy of St. Petersburg and provides a platform for local and national artists to showcase their talent.

Seasonal Programming: The theater typically offers a seasonal lineup of plays and musicals, so you can choose from a variety of performances throughout the year.

Check the Schedule: Be sure to check the theater's schedule for upcoming productions, ticket information, and any additional details about the show you wish to attend.

Attending live theater at American Stage Theatre is an enriching and enjoyable experience, allowing you to immerse yourself in the world of storytelling and artistic expression. It's an ideal destination for theater enthusiasts, those seeking cultural enrichment, and anyone looking to enjoy a night of live entertainment.

12.Enjoy a show at the Palladium Theater.

Enjoying a show at the Palladium Theater in St. Petersburg, Florida, is a cultural and artistic experience. Here's what you can expect when you attend a performance at this renowned theater:

Diverse Performances: The Palladium Theater hosts a wide range of live performances, including concerts, jazz, classical music, dance, comedy shows, theatrical productions, and more. You can choose from an array of artistic and entertainment options.

Historic Venue: The theater is located in the historic setting of the former First Church of Christ, Scientist, and it retains its architectural charm. The building itself adds to the overall ambiance and character of the performances.

Acoustic Excellence: The Palladium is known for its exceptional acoustics, providing a superb audio-visual experience. Musicians, performers, and audiences alike appreciate the outstanding sound quality.

Intimate Setting: The theater offers an intimate and cozy atmosphere, allowing for a close connection between the performers and the audience. It's an ideal space to enjoy live music and entertainment.

Variety of Genres: The Palladium hosts performances spanning various musical genres, from classical and jazz to blues, rock, and world music. You can experience a diverse array of musical traditions and styles.

Theatrical Productions: In addition to music, the Palladium often features theatrical productions, including plays, musicals, and dramatic performances, offering a well-rounded cultural experience.

Dance Performances: Enjoy the grace and artistry of professional dance companies that frequently perform at the Palladium. Dance performances range from classical ballet to contemporary and world dance.

Comedy Acts: The theater also hosts stand-up comedy shows, providing evenings of laughter and entertainment.

Educational Programs: The Palladium offers educational programs, lectures, and workshops that promote a greater understanding of the performing arts and culture.

Special Events: Check the Palladium's calendar for special events, including music festivals, tribute performances, and themed concerts. These events often provide unique and memorable experiences.

Community Engagement: The Palladium actively engages with the local community by collaborating with schools, organizations, and cultural institutions to promote the performing arts and artistic enrichment.

Artistic Inspiration: Attending a show at the Palladium can be an inspiring experience, whether you're a musician, actor, dancer, or simply an enthusiast of the performing arts.

Lobby and Intermission: The theater's lobby and facilities provide a pleasant space to mingle with fellow attendees during intermissions and before and after the show.

Check the Schedule: Be sure to check the Palladium's schedule for upcoming performances, ticket information, and any additional details about the show you wish to attend.

Attending a show at the Palladium Theater is a cultural highlight in St. Petersburg, providing you with an opportunity to enjoy world-class entertainment in an intimate and historic setting. Be sure to check the theater's website for show schedules, ticket information, and any special events or programs that may coincide with your visit.

13.Attend the St. Petersburg Shakespeare Festival.

Attending the St. Petersburg Shakespeare Festival is a wonderful opportunity to immerse yourself in the timeless works of William Shakespeare and enjoy the magic of live theater. Here's what you can expect when you attend this annual festival:

Shakespearean Performances: The St. Petersburg Shakespeare Festival features a selection of Shakespeare's most beloved plays, offering a chance to experience the Bard's iconic works brought to life on stage.

Travel to St. Petersburg Florida

Outdoor Venues: The festival often takes place in scenic outdoor venues, providing a unique and open-air setting for the performances. It's an opportunity to enjoy Shakespeare's masterpieces in a beautiful natural environment.

Professional and Community Performers: The festival typically includes performances by both professional actors and local community theater groups, contributing to a diverse and collaborative theatrical experience.

Variety of Plays: Each festival may feature a different set of Shakespearean plays, offering a range of genres, from tragedies like "Hamlet" and "Macbeth" to comedies like "A Midsummer Night's Dream" and "Twelfth Night."

Educational Programs: The festival often includes educational programs, workshops, and lectures related to Shakespeare and his works. These programs can enhance your understanding and appreciation of the plays.

Family-Friendly Events: Some festival editions include family-friendly events and adaptations of Shakespeare's plays designed to engage and entertain younger audiences.

Cultural Experience: The festival provides a cultural and artistic experience, allowing you to connect with the timeless themes, characters, and language of Shakespeare's works.

Picnicking: Many attendees enjoy picnicking before or during the performances, adding to the relaxed and communal atmosphere of the festival.

Community Engagement: The festival actively engages with the local community, promoting a love for theater and Shakespeare's legacy through outreach programs and partnerships with schools and organizations.

Special Events: Keep an eye on the festival's schedule for special events, including pre-show discussions, behind-the-scenes tours, and themed activities that enrich the overall experience.

Ticketing Information: Be sure to check the festival's website for ticketing information, showtimes, and any additional details about the specific plays and events featured in the festival's lineup.

Attending the St. Petersburg Shakespeare Festival offers an opportunity to celebrate the enduring brilliance of Shakespeare's works and enjoy the arts in a unique and enchanting setting. Whether you're a dedicated Shakespeare enthusiast or new to his plays, the festival provides a memorable and cultural experience that bridges the past and the present.

14.Take a guided mural tour.

Taking a guided mural tour in St. Petersburg, Florida, is a fantastic way to explore the vibrant and ever-evolving street art scene in the city. Here's what you can expect when you embark on a mural tour:

Local Artistic Expression: St. Petersburg is known for its thriving street art community. A mural tour allows you to witness the creativity and expression of local and international artists who have contributed to the city's artistic landscape.

Guided Experience: When you join a mural tour, you'll typically have a knowledgeable guide who can provide insights into the art, the artists, and the significance of each mural. They may share stories about the creative process, the artists' inspirations, and the cultural impact of the murals.

Varied Styles: St. Petersburg's mural scene is characterized by a diverse array of artistic styles, from realistic and figurative art to abstract and graffiti-inspired works. The tour will expose you to a wide spectrum of creative approaches.

Historical and Cultural Context: Mural tours often provide historical and cultural context, allowing you to better understand the social, political, and artistic influences that have shaped the murals in the city.

Interactive Elements: Some mural tours include interactive elements, such as opportunities to meet artists, participate in street art workshops, or even contribute to collaborative mural projects.

Photography Opportunities: Murals provide excellent photo opportunities, and many tours allow you to capture the art and your experience through photography.

Community Engagement: Mural tours may emphasize the role of street art in community engagement, urban revitalization, and cultural expression.

Evolving Art: The mural scene in St. Petersburg is dynamic, with new murals constantly appearing and old ones evolving. The tour can showcase the ever-changing nature of street art.

Local Insights: Your guide may provide local insights into the city's neighborhoods and how murals have become integral to the cultural identity of St. Petersburg.

Artistic Hotspots: The tour can lead you to artistic hotspots and neighborhoods where you'll find concentrations of murals, street art studios, and galleries.

Check the Schedule: Be sure to check the schedule and availability of mural tours in St. Petersburg, as they may be offered on specific days or as part of special events or festivals.

A guided mural tour is a dynamic and artistic journey that allows you to connect with the city's culture, creativity, and community spirit. It's an ideal experience for art enthusiasts, photographers, and anyone interested in exploring the dynamic world of street art in St. Petersburg.

15.Discover the Duncan McClellan Gallery.

Discovering the Duncan McClellan Gallery in St. Petersburg, Florida, is an opportunity to explore the world of contemporary glass art. Here's what you can expect when you visit this gallery:

Contemporary Glass Art: The Duncan McClellan Gallery is dedicated to contemporary glass art. You'll encounter an impressive collection of glass sculptures, blown glass creations, and other glass artworks crafted by renowned artists from around the world.

Diverse Styles: The gallery showcases a wide variety of glass art styles and techniques, from traditional and functional glassware to innovative and experimental glass forms. You'll have the chance to appreciate the creative breadth of this medium.

Glassblowing Demonstrations: The gallery often hosts live glassblowing demonstrations, allowing you to witness the mesmerizing process of shaping molten glass into intricate and beautiful forms. These demonstrations offer insight into the artistic techniques involved in glassblowing.

Permanent and Rotating Exhibits: The gallery features both permanent collections and rotating exhibits, ensuring that each visit provides a fresh and dynamic experience with different artists and themes.

Educational Programs: The Duncan McClellan Gallery offers educational programs, workshops, and lectures for visitors of all ages. These programs help deepen your understanding of the art form and its creative process.

Artistic Inspiration: Whether you're an artist or an art enthusiast, a visit to the gallery can be an inspiring experience, exposing you to the limitless possibilities of glass as an artistic medium.

Special Events: Check the gallery's calendar for special events, art openings, and exhibitions that may coincide with your visit. These events often provide opportunities to meet artists and engage with the local art community.

Art Shop: The gallery's gift shop offers unique glass art pieces, jewelry, books, and glass-related gifts. It's a great place to find artistic souvenirs or one-of-a-kind gifts.

Community Engagement: The Duncan McClellan Gallery is actively involved in the local art community, collaborating with artists, schools, and organizations to promote glass art and creative expression.

Architectural Setting: The gallery is housed in an architecturally interesting building, providing an engaging and aesthetically pleasing environment to appreciate the glass art.

Visiting the Duncan McClellan Gallery offers a visually captivating and inspiring experience, allowing you to immerse yourself in the world of glass art and explore the creative expressions of contemporary artists. Be sure to check the gallery's operating hours, current exhibits, and any special events or programs that may be taking place during your visit.

16. Visit Great Explorations Children's Museum.

Visiting Great Explorations Children's Museum in St. Petersburg, Florida, is a delightful and educational experience for both children and families. Here's what you can expect when you explore this interactive and engaging museum:

Hands-On Learning: Great Explorations Children's Museum is designed to be a hands-on learning environment. Children can actively engage with the exhibits, making learning fun and interactive.

Interactive Exhibits: The museum features a wide range of interactive exhibits covering various themes, including science, technology, arts, and culture. These exhibits are designed to stimulate creativity and curiosity.

Art and Creativity: Children can explore their artistic side through activities like painting, drawing, and crafting. Art-based exhibits encourage self-expression and creativity.

Science and Discovery: The museum offers science-themed exhibits that allow children to experiment, learn about the natural world, and develop critical thinking skills.

Outdoor Play Area: Many children's museums have outdoor play areas, and Great Explorations is no exception. The outdoor space often includes play structures, gardens, and additional hands-on activities.

Early Learning: The museum caters to children of all ages, including infants and toddlers. You'll find age-appropriate activities and play areas designed to support early childhood development.

Educational Programs: Great Explorations offers educational programs, workshops, and classes that provide additional learning opportunities for children and families. These programs often focus on science, arts, and cultural topics.

Special Events: Check the museum's calendar for special events, including themed days, workshops, and interactive performances that add excitement to the visit.

Birthday Parties: Many children's museums offer birthday party packages, providing a unique and fun way to celebrate a child's special day.

Gift Shop: The museum's gift shop often sells educational toys, books, and unique items related to the themes and activities found in the museum.

Community Engagement: Great Explorations Children's Museum actively engages with the local community by collaborating with schools, educators, and families to promote early childhood education and hands-on learning.

Check the Schedule: Be sure to check the museum's schedule, operating hours, admission fees, and any upcoming events or programs that may enhance your visit.

Visiting Great Explorations Children's Museum is a wonderful opportunity for children to play, learn, and explore in a stimulating and supportive environment. It encourages curiosity, creativity, and the development of important skills. Whether you're a local or a visitor, the museum provides a memorable and educational experience for families with young children.

17.Explore the Suncoast Seabird Sanctuary.

Exploring the Suncoast Seabird Sanctuary in St. Petersburg, Florida, is an opportunity to connect with nature and learn about the conservation efforts dedicated to the well-being of coastal and marine birds. Here's what you can expect when you visit this avian rescue and education facility:

Avian Rehabilitation: The Suncoast Seabird Sanctuary is primarily known for its avian rehabilitation efforts. The sanctuary rescues and rehabilitates injured, sick, and orphaned birds, with the goal of releasing them back into the wild once they are healthy.

Variety of Bird Species: You'll encounter a wide variety of bird species at the sanctuary, including pelicans, herons, eagles, owls, gulls, and more. The sanctuary provides a home to both local and migratory birds.

Education: The sanctuary is committed to education and conservation. Visitors can learn about the importance of preserving coastal and marine bird habitats, the challenges these birds face, and what individuals can do to help.

Observation and Photography: The sanctuary offers opportunities for bird watching and photography, allowing you to observe the birds in a natural setting and capture their beauty.

Outdoor Environment: The sanctuary is typically located in a scenic, natural environment near the coast. It provides a peaceful and serene setting for both bird enthusiasts and nature lovers.

Volunteer Opportunities: Many visitors are inspired to become volunteers at the Suncoast Seabird Sanctuary. Volunteering can involve tasks like bird care, habitat maintenance, and public education.

Gift Shop: The sanctuary's gift shop often sells bird-related merchandise, books, and educational materials, with proceeds supporting the organization's conservation efforts.

Community Engagement: The Suncoast Seabird Sanctuary is actively involved in the local community, working with schools, environmental groups, and volunteers to promote bird conservation and education.

Check the Schedule: Be sure to check the sanctuary's schedule, operating hours, and any special events or guided tours that may be available during your visit.

Visiting the Suncoast Seabird Sanctuary is an opportunity to appreciate the beauty of coastal and marine birds, learn about their importance in the ecosystem, and support efforts to protect and rehabilitate them. It's a meaningful and educational experience for bird enthusiasts and nature lovers of all ages.

18.Enjoy the Boyd Hill Nature Preserve.

Enjoying the Boyd Hill Nature Preserve in St. Petersburg, Florida, is a serene and immersive experience in natural beauty and wildlife. Here's what you can expect when you explore this expansive and biodiverse nature preserve:

Trails and Hiking: The Boyd Hill Nature Preserve offers a network of well-maintained trails that wind through various natural habitats. You can enjoy leisurely walks or more challenging hikes, depending on your preference.

Rich Biodiversity: The preserve is home to a diverse array of plant and animal species. Birdwatchers, in particular, will find plenty of opportunities to spot local and migratory birds. Other wildlife includes turtles, alligators, and various aquatic life.

Educational Center: The Boyd Hill Nature Preserve often features an educational center where visitors can learn about the local flora and fauna. The center may include interactive exhibits, informative displays, and knowledgeable staff to answer questions.

Environmental Programs: The preserve frequently offers environmental education programs and guided nature walks led by naturalists. These programs provide in-depth information about the ecosystem and its conservation.

Lake Maggiore: The preserve is situated around Lake Maggiore, which is a picturesque setting for picnics, wildlife observation, and water-based activities such as kayaking and canoeing. You can often rent watercraft at the preserve.

Garden Areas: Some parts of the preserve feature beautifully landscaped gardens, including a butterfly garden and a wildflower garden. These areas offer opportunities for relaxation and photography.

Sunset Views: Boyd Hill Nature Preserve is known for its stunning sunset views. Many visitors choose to visit in the late afternoon to witness the sun setting over the lake.

Photography: With its diverse ecosystems and abundant wildlife, the preserve provides excellent opportunities for nature photography.

Community Engagement: The Boyd Hill Nature Preserve actively engages with the local community through environmental initiatives, volunteer opportunities, and educational outreach.

Special Events: Check the preserve's schedule for special events, nature-themed workshops, and nature-themed festivals that may coincide with your visit.

Facilities: The preserve often provides facilities such as picnic areas, restrooms, and shaded pavilions, making it a convenient destination for families and outdoor enthusiasts.

Check the Schedule: Be sure to check the Boyd Hill Nature Preserve's operating hours and any seasonal considerations, such as insect repellent needs, and to inquire about any special events or programs.

Exploring the Boyd Hill Nature Preserve is an opportunity to connect with the natural world and experience the serenity of unspoiled landscapes in an urban setting. Whether you're interested in hiking, birdwatching, or simply enjoying the tranquility of nature, the preserve provides a peaceful and enriching experience for visitors of all ages.

19.Go birdwatching at Fort De Soto Park.

Birdwatching at Fort De Soto Park, located near St. Petersburg, Florida, is a rewarding experience due to its diverse ecosystems and rich birdlife. Here's what you can expect when you visit this birdwatching hotspot:

Bird Diversity: Fort De Soto Park is renowned for its rich bird diversity, attracting both resident and migratory species. Birdwatchers have the opportunity to spot a wide range of birds, from shorebirds and waders to raptors and songbirds.

Prime Birding Locations: The park offers various prime birdwatching locations, including North Beach, East Beach, and the Arrowhead Picnic Area, where you can observe different bird species in their natural habitats.

Migratory Birds: The park is situated along the Great Florida Birding and Wildlife Trail and serves as a crucial stopover for migratory birds, making it an excellent location for observing seasonal bird migrations.

Birding Platforms and Trails: Fort De Soto Park features designated birding platforms and trails that provide optimal viewing opportunities for both seasoned and novice birdwatchers.

Photography: The park's scenic beauty and diverse birdlife offer great opportunities for bird photography, allowing you to capture the beauty of the birds and their surroundings.

Educational Signage: Look for educational signs along the trails that provide information about the park's bird species, habitats, and conservation efforts.

Quiet and Peaceful: The park offers a peaceful and unspoiled natural environment that encourages a sense of tranquility and mindfulness as you observe the birds.

Picnicking and Recreation: Fort De Soto Park offers amenities like picnic areas, restroom facilities, and recreational opportunities for a full day of outdoor enjoyment.

Birding Events: Check for birding events and guided tours that may be organized by local birdwatching groups or the park itself, providing expert guidance and enhancing your birdwatching experience.

Community Engagement: The park actively engages with the local community through birdwatching clubs, environmental initiatives, and educational programs focused on bird conservation.

Visitor Center: Visit the park's visitor center for additional information on birdwatching, local wildlife, and park amenities.

Check the Schedule: Be sure to check the park's operating hours, any entrance fees, and consider the best times of the year for birdwatching based on migratory patterns and bird activity.

Birdwatching at Fort De Soto Park offers an opportunity to connect with the natural world, appreciate the beauty of avian diversity, and engage in the peaceful practice of birdwatching. Whether you're a seasoned birder or a beginner, the park provides a beautiful and enriching experience for nature enthusiasts and birdwatchers of all levels.

20. Visit Weedon Island Preserve.

Visiting Weedon Island Preserve in St. Petersburg, Florida, is a wonderful way to immerse yourself in a pristine natural environment and explore the unique ecosystems of this protected area. Here's what you can expect when you visit this beautiful preserve:

Natural Beauty: Weedon Island Preserve is known for its stunning natural beauty, featuring lush landscapes, wetlands, and mangrove forests. The preserve offers a peaceful escape into nature.

Travel to St. Petersburg Florida

Boardwalks and Trails: The preserve offers a network of boardwalks and trails that wind through different ecosystems, allowing you to explore the diverse flora and fauna. These paths provide a serene setting for hiking and wildlife observation.

Biodiversity: Weedon Island is rich in biodiversity, and you can expect to encounter various wildlife species, including birds, fish, reptiles, and marine life. It's a prime location for birdwatching and wildlife photography.

Canoe and Kayak Trails: The preserve features water trails suitable for kayaking and canoeing. Paddling through the calm waters of the bay and estuaries is a unique way to explore the environment and observe wildlife.

Educational Center: The Weedon Island Preserve Cultural and Natural History Center offers educational exhibits and information about the natural and cultural history of the area. It's a great place to start your visit and learn more about the preserve.

Educational Programs: The center often hosts educational programs, guided nature walks, and workshops that provide insights into the local ecosystem, history, and conservation efforts.

Archaeological Sites: Weedon Island is home to archaeological sites that date back thousands of years. You can learn about the region's indigenous history and cultural significance.

Environmental Stewardship: The preserve actively engages in environmental stewardship and conservation efforts, working with local communities to protect the natural resources of the area.

Community Engagement: Weedon Island Preserve often collaborates with local schools, environmental groups, and researchers, fostering community engagement and supporting environmental education.

Picnicking and Relaxation: The preserve provides picnic areas and rest spots, allowing you to relax and enjoy the serene surroundings.

Check the Schedule: Be sure to check the preserve's operating hours, any admission fees, and any guided tours or special events that may enhance your visit.

Visiting Weedon Island Preserve is an opportunity to appreciate the beauty of natural landscapes, connect with local ecosystems, and engage in outdoor activities like hiking, kayaking, and wildlife observation. Whether you're a nature enthusiast, an explorer, or someone looking for a peaceful retreat into nature, the preserve offers a serene and educational experience for visitors of all ages.

21.Explore Sawgrass Lake Park.

Exploring Sawgrass Lake Park in St. Petersburg, Florida, is an opportunity to connect with the unique and diverse ecosystems of a protected natural area. Here's what you can expect when you visit this beautiful park:

Wetland Ecosystems: Sawgrass Lake Park is known for its extensive wetland ecosystems, including freshwater marshes and swamps. These habitats are home to various plant and animal species, making it a prime location for nature enthusiasts and birdwatchers.

Boardwalks and Trails: The park offers a network of boardwalks and trails that wind through the wetlands, providing opportunities for hiking and wildlife observation. The raised boardwalks allow you to explore the marshes while minimizing impact on the delicate ecosystem.

Biodiversity: Sawgrass Lake Park is teeming with biodiversity. You can expect to see a wide range of wildlife, including birds, reptiles, amphibians, and insects. The park is especially known for its birdwatching opportunities, and it's a designated site on the Great Florida Birding Trail.

Educational Signage: Throughout the park, you'll find informative signage that provides details about the flora, fauna, and the significance of the wetland ecosystem. These signs offer valuable insights into the natural world.

Birdwatching: Birdwatchers will be in their element at Sawgrass Lake Park. It's an excellent location to observe a variety of bird species, including wading birds, songbirds, and raptors. Bring your binoculars and bird field guide.

Photography: The park's scenic beauty and diverse wildlife make it a prime location for nature photography. You can capture the beauty of the wetland habitats and their inhabitants.

Educational Programs: Sawgrass Lake Park often hosts educational programs, guided nature walks, and workshops that delve into the natural history and conservation efforts related to the park's ecosystems.

Community Engagement: The park actively engages with the local community, collaborating with schools, environmental organizations, and volunteers to promote environmental education and stewardship.

Picnic Areas and Observation Towers: The park provides picnic areas and observation towers, allowing you to relax and enjoy the natural surroundings. Observation towers offer elevated views of the wetlands.

Check the Schedule: Be sure to check the park's operating hours, any admission fees, and any guided tours or special events that may coincide with your visit.

Exploring Sawgrass Lake Park is an opportunity to connect with the beauty and importance of wetland ecosystems, observe wildlife in their natural habitats, and appreciate the tranquil ambiance of a protected natural area. Whether you're an avid naturalist, a bird enthusiast, or simply seeking a peaceful retreat into nature, the park provides a serene and educational experience for visitors of all ages.

22.Go hiking at Brooker Creek Preserve.

Going hiking at Brooker Creek Preserve in Tarpon Springs, Florida, is a chance to explore the beauty of a protected natural area and connect with the diverse ecosystems of the region. Here's what you can expect when you visit this pristine preserve for a hiking adventure:

Hiking Trails: Brooker Creek Preserve offers a network of hiking trails that wind through the natural habitats of the preserve. These trails are well-marked and provide a range of hiking options for different skill levels and preferences.

Natural Beauty: The preserve features a diverse landscape that includes forests, wetlands, pine flatwoods, and open prairies. You'll have the opportunity to immerse yourself in the natural beauty of the area.

Biodiversity: The preserve is home to a wide variety of plant and animal species, making it an excellent location for wildlife observation and nature appreciation. Keep an eye out for native flora and fauna along the trails.

Birdwatching: Birdwatchers will find plenty of opportunities to spot local and migratory bird species. The preserve is known for its birdwatching potential, and you may encounter songbirds, raptors, and waterfowl.

Educational Signage: Along the hiking trails, you'll often find educational signage that provides information about the natural history, ecosystems, and wildlife of the preserve. These signs offer valuable insights into the surroundings.

Picnic Areas: The preserve typically offers designated picnic areas and rest spots, allowing you to take a break, enjoy a meal, and appreciate the serene natural setting.

Photography: With its diverse landscapes and wildlife, Brooker Creek Preserve provides excellent opportunities for nature photography. Capture the beauty of the preserve's ecosystems and inhabitants.

Community Engagement: The preserve actively engages with the local community through educational programs, environmental initiatives, and volunteer opportunities aimed at promoting conservation and environmental education.

Special Events: Check the preserve's schedule for special events, guided hikes, and nature-themed workshops that may enhance your hiking experience.

Visitor Center: Visit the preserve's visitor center for additional information on the hiking trails, local wildlife, and amenities.

Check the Schedule: Be sure to check the preserve's operating hours, any admission fees, and any trail conditions or restrictions that may apply during your visit.

Hiking at Brooker Creek Preserve offers a chance to appreciate the beauty and importance of natural landscapes, connect with the local ecosystems, and engage in an outdoor adventure. Whether you're an experienced hiker, a nature enthusiast, or someone seeking a tranquil escape into the wilderness, the preserve provides a serene and educational experience for hikers of all levels.

23.Enjoy the Suncoast Primate Sanctuary.

Visiting the Suncoast Primate Sanctuary in Palm Harbor, Florida, is an opportunity to connect with and learn about a variety of primate species and support the sanctuary's mission of providing a safe and caring environment for these animals. Here's what you can expect when you visit this primate sanctuary:

Primate Observation: The Suncoast Primate Sanctuary is home to a diverse group of primates, including capuchin monkeys, macaques, and chimpanzees. You can observe and learn about these fascinating animals up close.

Educational Experience: The sanctuary often provides educational information about the primates, their habitats, behaviors, and the challenges they face in the wild. You can gain a better understanding of the importance of primate conservation.

Animal Welfare: The sanctuary is dedicated to providing a safe and caring environment for the primates, many of whom have been rescued from various situations. Visitors can learn about the sanctuary's commitment to animal welfare.

Guided Tours: Some visits may include guided tours that offer insights into the individual stories and personalities of the primates in the sanctuary's care.

Photo Opportunities: The sanctuary typically allows visitors to take photographs of the primates, providing opportunities to capture memorable moments during your visit.

Community Engagement: The Suncoast Primate Sanctuary actively engages with the local community through educational programs, outreach efforts, and collaborations with schools and organizations.

Gift Shop: The sanctuary often features a gift shop where you can find primate-themed merchandise, educational materials, and souvenirs. Proceeds from purchases often support the sanctuary's work.

Events and Fundraisers: Check the sanctuary's schedule for special events, fundraisers, and programs that may coincide with your visit and provide additional ways to support their mission.

Picnic Areas: Some sanctuaries provide picnic areas where you can enjoy a meal while surrounded by the serene environment of the sanctuary.

Check the Schedule: Be sure to check the sanctuary's operating hours, admission fees, and any specific guidelines or regulations that apply to your visit.

Visiting the Suncoast Primate Sanctuary offers an opportunity to connect with primates, learn about their conservation, and support the sanctuary's efforts to provide a safe and caring environment for these animals. Whether you're an animal lover, an advocate for wildlife conservation, or someone seeking a unique and educational experience, the sanctuary provides an engaging and memorable visit for visitors of all ages.

24. Visit Heritage Village.

Visiting Heritage Village in Largo, Florida, is a journey back in time to explore a meticulously preserved collection of historical buildings and exhibits that showcase the history and culture of the region. Here's what you can expect when you explore this living history museum:

Historical Buildings: Heritage Village features a collection of historic buildings that have been carefully relocated and preserved. These buildings include homes, schools, churches, and businesses, representing different periods in Florida's history.

Living History: The museum often employs interpreters and volunteers who dress in period-appropriate clothing and engage in "living history" demonstrations. These demonstrations bring history to life and offer insights into daily life in the past.

Exhibits and Artifacts: In addition to the buildings, Heritage Village houses exhibits and displays that feature artifacts, documents, and photographs from the area's history. These exhibits provide a broader context for the historical structures.

Educational Programs: The museum frequently offers educational programs, workshops, and guided tours that delve into specific aspects of local history. These programs can enhance your understanding of the region's heritage.

Special Events: Check the museum's calendar for special events and themed days that may coincide with your visit. These events often include demonstrations, reenactments, and family-friendly activities.

Historical Gardens: Some historical homes on the property feature beautifully landscaped gardens that reflect the gardening practices of the time. Take a leisurely stroll through these gardens to appreciate the horticultural history.

Picnic Areas: Heritage Village often provides picnic areas, making it a great place for a relaxing outdoor meal.

Gift Shop: The museum typically has a gift shop where you can find historical books, souvenirs, and unique items related to the region's history.

Community Engagement: Heritage Village actively engages with the local community through partnerships with schools, historical societies, and volunteers who help preserve and promote the area's heritage.

Check the Schedule: Be sure to check the museum's operating hours, admission fees, and any upcoming programs or events that may enhance your visit.

Visiting Heritage Village offers a unique and immersive opportunity to step into the past and explore the history and culture of the region. Whether you're a history enthusiast, a student, or someone looking to connect with the heritage of the area, the museum provides an educational and enriching experience for visitors of all ages.

25.Explore the Florida Botanical Gardens.

Exploring the Florida Botanical Gardens in Largo, Florida, is a delightful journey through beautifully landscaped gardens and natural surroundings. Here's what you can expect when you visit this botanical haven:

Lush Gardens: The Florida Botanical Gardens feature a diverse range of gardens, each with its own unique theme and plant collections. You can explore gardens such as the Tropical Fruit Garden, Butterfly Garden, Herb Garden, and many others.

Native and Exotic Plants: The gardens showcase a wide variety of plants, including both native Florida species and exotic plants from around the world. This diversity provides a rich and educational experience for visitors.

Walking Trails: The gardens offer well-maintained walking paths and trails that wind through the different garden areas. These paths allow you to leisurely explore the gardens and enjoy the natural beauty.

Butterfly Garden: The Butterfly Garden is a highlight, designed to attract and support native butterfly species. It's a tranquil spot for observing these colorful insects in their natural habitat.

Educational Signage: Throughout the gardens, you'll find educational signage providing information about the plants, ecosystems, and conservation efforts. These signs enhance your understanding of the botanical displays.

Scenic Beauty: The gardens are known for their scenic beauty, offering opportunities for photography, nature appreciation, and relaxation in a serene environment.

Special Events: Check the gardens' calendar for special events, plant sales, workshops, and educational programs that may coincide with your visit.

Art Installations: Some botanical gardens feature art installations, sculptures, or outdoor art displays that add an artistic dimension to your visit.

Picnic Areas: Many botanical gardens provide picnic areas, allowing you to enjoy a meal surrounded by the beauty of the gardens.

Gift Shop: The gardens often have a gift shop where you can find plant-related merchandise, gardening supplies, and unique items as souvenirs.

Community Engagement: The Florida Botanical Gardens engage with the local community through partnerships with schools, horticultural societies, and volunteers who help maintain and promote the gardens.

Check the Schedule: Be sure to check the gardens' operating hours, admission fees, and any seasonal considerations, such as blooming seasons for specific plant collections.

Visiting the Florida Botanical Gardens offers a chance to connect with the beauty of natural landscapes, appreciate a wide variety of plants, and immerse yourself in the tranquility of well-designed gardens. Whether you're a botany enthusiast, a gardening enthusiast, or someone seeking a serene outdoor experience, the gardens provide an enriching and peaceful visit for visitors of all ages.

26.Discover the Largo Central Park Nature Preserve.

Discovering the Largo Central Park Nature Preserve in Largo, Florida, is an opportunity to connect with the natural environment, explore native habitats, and enjoy outdoor activities. Here's what you can expect when you visit this serene nature preserve:

Native Ecosystems: Largo Central Park Nature Preserve is home to a variety of native Florida ecosystems, including wetlands, forests, and meadows. These ecosystems are carefully preserved to provide a natural and biodiverse environment.

Walking Trails: The preserve features a network of walking trails and boardwalks that allow visitors to explore the different habitats. These trails are suitable for both leisurely strolls and more active hiking.

Wildlife Observation: The preserve is an excellent location for observing local wildlife, including birds, reptiles, amphibians, and other native species. Birdwatching is a popular activity, and you may spot a variety of avian species.

Educational Signage: Along the trails, you'll often find informative signage that offers details about the flora, fauna, and ecosystems of the preserve. These signs provide educational insights for visitors.

Ponds and Lakes: The preserve is home to ponds and lakes, which provide scenic views and opportunities for fishing, kayaking, and wildlife observation.

Picnicking: The park often provides picnic areas, making it a great place for a relaxing outdoor meal with family or friends.

Art Installations: Some nature preserves feature outdoor art installations, sculptures, or interpretive art that adds an artistic and cultural dimension to your visit.

Community Engagement: Largo Central Park Nature Preserve actively engages with the local community through environmental initiatives, educational programs, and volunteer opportunities.

Special Events: Check the preserve's calendar for special events, guided nature walks, and educational programs that may coincide with your visit.

Check the Schedule: Be sure to check the preserve's operating hours, any admission fees, and any seasonal considerations, such as insect repellent needs and wildlife activity patterns.

Visiting Largo Central Park Nature Preserve offers a chance to connect with the natural world, appreciate native ecosystems, and engage in outdoor activities in a serene and protected environment. Whether you're a nature enthusiast, a hiker, or someone seeking a peaceful retreat into nature, the preserve provides an educational and enjoyable experience for visitors of all ages.

27.Attend a Tampa Bay Rowdies soccer game.

Attending a Tampa Bay Rowdies soccer game is an exciting sports experience for fans and newcomers alike. Here's what you can expect when you attend a Rowdies match:

Professional Soccer: The Tampa Bay Rowdies are a professional soccer team that competes in the United Soccer League (USL), a top-level soccer league in the United States.

Game Atmosphere: Rowdies games are known for their lively and passionate fan atmosphere. You can expect to hear chants, cheers, and drumbeats as fans support their team throughout the match.

Al Lang Stadium: The team typically plays its home games at Al Lang Stadium in St. Petersburg, Florida. The stadium offers excellent views of the field, and its waterfront location provides a scenic backdrop for soccer action.

Tailgating and Pre-game Activities: Many fans engage in pre-game activities like tailgating, where you can join in the festivities with fellow fans, enjoy food and drinks, and build excitement for the game.

Food and Beverages: The stadium usually offers a variety of food and beverage options, including traditional stadium fare like hot dogs, popcorn, and cold drinks.

Merchandise: Team merchandise, including jerseys, scarves, and other memorabilia, is often available for purchase at the stadium, allowing you to support the team in style.

Entertainment: Rowdies games often feature halftime entertainment, contests, and special events, making the experience even more enjoyable for fans of all ages.

Family-Friendly: The Rowdies aim to create a family-friendly environment, so attending games with children can be a fun and wholesome experience.

Community Engagement: The team actively engages with the local community through youth programs, soccer clinics, and outreach initiatives.

Check the Schedule: Be sure to check the Tampa Bay Rowdies' schedule, ticket availability, and any special promotions or theme nights that may be happening on the day you plan to attend a game.

Attending a Tampa Bay Rowdies soccer game is an opportunity to enjoy professional soccer in a spirited and lively atmosphere. Whether you're a soccer enthusiast, a sports fan, or simply looking for an exciting and entertaining outing, a Rowdies game provides an unforgettable sports experience in the Tampa Bay area.

28.Catch a Tampa Bay Rays baseball game.

Attending a Tampa Bay Rays baseball game is a classic American sports experience. Here's what you can expect when you catch a Rays game at Tropicana Field in St. Petersburg, Florida:

Major League Baseball: The Tampa Bay Rays are a Major League Baseball (MLB) team, competing in the American League. You'll witness high-level baseball featuring some of the best players in the sport.

Tropicana Field: The Rays play their home games at Tropicana Field, an indoor stadium that provides a climate-controlled environment, protecting fans from the Florida heat and occasional rain.

Game Atmosphere: Rays games have a vibrant and energetic atmosphere with dedicated fans known as "Rays Republic." You can expect the excitement of baseball with crowd cheers, music, and team spirit.

Food and Drinks: Tropicana Field offers a wide variety of concessions and dining options. You can enjoy classic ballpark snacks like hot dogs, peanuts, and popcorn, as well as specialty food items.

Merchandise: The stadium typically has team merchandise shops where you can purchase Rays jerseys, caps, and other memorabilia to show your support for the team.

Family-Friendly: Rays games are family-friendly, and the team often hosts special family events and activities. There are designated areas for children to enjoy games and interactive features.

Entertainment: In addition to the game, Rays games often feature entertainment between innings, including trivia, contests, and giveaways.

Community Engagement: The Tampa Bay Rays are involved in community outreach and support various charitable initiatives. You can learn about their community involvement during your visit.

Check the Schedule: Be sure to check the Tampa Bay Rays' schedule, ticket availability, and any special promotions or theme nights happening on the day you plan to attend a game.

Attending a Tampa Bay Rays baseball game is a classic American sports experience, and it's an opportunity to enjoy the excitement of Major League Baseball. Whether you're a die-hard baseball fan, a sports enthusiast, or just looking for a fun and memorable outing, a Rays game provides a great way to enjoy America's pastime in the Tampa Bay area.

29.Explore Tropicana Field.

Exploring Tropicana Field, also known as "The Trop," in St. Petersburg, Florida, is a chance to experience the home stadium of the Tampa Bay Rays and discover the unique features of this indoor baseball facility:

Game Days: Tropicana Field is the home stadium of the Tampa Bay Rays, a Major League Baseball (MLB) team. When the Rays are playing at home, you can attend a game to witness top-tier baseball action.

Indoor Stadium: Tropicana Field is known for being one of the few indoor MLB stadiums. Its fixed, translucent roof provides a climate-controlled environment, protecting fans from Florida's unpredictable weather.

Seating Options: The stadium offers a variety of seating options, including field-level seats, upper-level seating, and suites. You can choose the seating that best suits your preferences and budget.

Food and Beverage: Tropicana Field features a wide range of concessions and dining options. Enjoy classic ballpark fare like hot dogs, nachos, and peanuts, as well as specialty food items and local cuisine.

St. Petersburg Baseball Museum: The Ted Williams Museum and Hitters Hall of Fame, located within Tropicana Field, celebrates the history of baseball and honors the legendary Red Sox player, Ted Williams.

Rays Touch Tank: One of the unique features of the stadium is the Rays Touch Tank, which is home to cownose rays. Fans can touch and feed the rays during the game, offering an interactive and educational experience.

Team Merchandise: Explore the various merchandise shops within the stadium to find official Tampa Bay Rays gear, including jerseys, caps, and souvenirs.

Family-Friendly Activities: Tropicana Field offers family-friendly areas, such as the Rays Kid's Clubhouse, where children can enjoy games, activities, and interactive features.

Entertainment: In addition to the game, Rays games often feature entertainment between innings, including trivia, contests, and special promotions.

Community Engagement: The Tampa Bay Rays are involved in community outreach and often support charitable initiatives. You can learn more about their community involvement during your visit.

Guided Tours: Some stadiums offer guided tours, providing behind-the-scenes access and insights into the stadium's history, features, and operations.

Check the Schedule: Be sure to check the Tampa Bay Rays' schedule, ticket availability, and any special promotions or theme nights that may coincide with your visit.

Exploring Tropicana Field provides a unique opportunity to experience a Major League Baseball stadium with a distinctive indoor environment. Whether you're a baseball fan, a sports enthusiast, or someone looking for an entertaining and memorable outing, Tropicana Field offers an exciting experience in the heart of St. Petersburg, Florida.

30.Visit Al Lang Stadium for soccer games and events.

Visiting Al Lang Stadium in St. Petersburg, Florida, is an opportunity to enjoy soccer games and other events in a picturesque waterfront setting. Here's what you can expect when you visit this versatile and vibrant stadium:

Soccer Matches: Al Lang Stadium is home to the Tampa Bay Rowdies, a professional soccer team competing in the United Soccer League (USL). Attending Rowdies games offers an exciting and energetic sports experience.

Waterfront Location: The stadium's waterfront location along Tampa Bay provides stunning views and a refreshing breeze, making it a unique and picturesque setting for sports and events.

Game Atmosphere: Rowdies games are known for their lively and passionate fan atmosphere. You can expect to hear chants, cheers, and drumbeats as fans support their team throughout the match.

Food and Beverages: The stadium typically offers concessions and dining options, allowing you to enjoy a variety of food and beverages while watching the game.

Special Events: Al Lang Stadium hosts a variety of special events and concerts in addition to soccer matches. Be sure to check the schedule for upcoming events that may coincide with your visit.

Family-Friendly: The stadium aims to create a family-friendly environment, so attending games and events with children can be a fun and wholesome experience.

Merchandise: You'll often find merchandise shops at the stadium where you can purchase team-related gear and souvenirs.

Community Engagement: The stadium is involved in community outreach, supporting local initiatives and collaborating with organizations to promote soccer and community engagement.

Check the Schedule: Be sure to check Al Lang Stadium's schedule for upcoming soccer matches, events, ticket availability, and any special promotions or theme nights happening on the day you plan to attend.

Visiting Al Lang Stadium offers an opportunity to enjoy soccer, sports, and events in a scenic and vibrant setting. Whether you're a soccer enthusiast, a sports fan, or simply looking for an exciting and entertaining outing, Al Lang Stadium provides a memorable experience in St. Petersburg, Florida.

31.Enjoy a round of golf at local courses.

Enjoying a round of golf at local courses in St. Petersburg, Florida, is a popular outdoor activity in the region known for its beautiful weather and scenic golf courses. Here are a few local courses where you can tee off:

Mangrove Bay Golf Course: This city-owned, 18-hole course is located near downtown St. Petersburg. It offers challenging play and beautiful views of Tampa Bay.

Twin Brooks Golf Course: Situated within the scenic Meadowlawn neighborhood, Twin Brooks is a municipal golf course with an 18-hole layout that provides an enjoyable golfing experience.

St. Petersburg Country Club: This private club features a challenging 18-hole championship golf course surrounded by lush landscaping and scenic vistas.

Island Course at Innisbrook Resort: Located in nearby Palm Harbor, the Island Course is part of the renowned Innisbrook Resort and Golf Club. It features 18 holes and offers a premium golfing experience.

Feather Sound Country Club: Just a short drive from St. Petersburg, this private country club offers a challenging 18-hole golf course in a beautifully landscaped setting.

East Bay Golf Club: Situated in Largo, Florida, this 18-hole public golf course is known for its friendly atmosphere and well-maintained fairways and greens.

Cypress Links at Mangrove Bay: Located adjacent to Mangrove Bay Golf Course, Cypress Links is an executive 18-hole course designed for a quicker round of golf.

Lakewood Country Club: This private club offers a beautifully designed 18-hole golf course surrounded by lush vegetation and water features.

Bardmoor Golf and Tennis Club: Located in nearby Seminole, Florida, Bardmoor offers an 18-hole championship course known for its challenging play and scenic beauty.

Airco Golf Course: This public golf course, located in Clearwater, offers nine holes for those looking for a quick game of golf.

Before heading to any of these golf courses, be sure to check their schedules, availability, and any reservation requirements. Enjoying a round of golf in St. Petersburg allows you to experience the region's outdoor beauty while engaging in a popular and leisurely sporting activity.

32.Try stand-up paddleboarding on the Gulf.

Trying stand-up paddleboarding (SUP) on the Gulf of Mexico is a fantastic way to enjoy the water and the beautiful coastal scenery in the St. Petersburg area. Here's what you can expect when you take up this fun water activity:

Equipment Rental: You can typically rent paddleboards from local outfitters or water sports rental shops near the Gulf. They will provide you with the necessary equipment, including the paddleboard, paddle, and personal flotation device (PFD).

Instruction: If you're new to stand-up paddleboarding, many rental shops offer basic instructions and safety tips to ensure you have a safe and enjoyable experience.

Launch Sites: There are several launch sites along the Gulf Coast and within St. Petersburg where you can start your paddleboarding adventure. Some popular options include the St. Pete Beach area, Fort De Soto Park, and various waterfront parks and marinas.

Scenic Views: As you paddle along the Gulf, you'll have the opportunity to take in breathtaking views of the coastline, the crystal-clear waters, and the natural beauty of the Gulf of Mexico.

Wildlife Viewing: Keep an eye out for marine life, as you may spot dolphins, manatees, and various bird species while paddling in the Gulf.

Variety of Experiences: Whether you prefer a calm and leisurely paddle along the shoreline or a more adventurous journey out to the open water, there are options to suit your comfort level and experience.

Fitness and Relaxation: Stand-up paddleboarding provides a great workout for your core muscles and balance, but it's also a relaxing and peaceful way to enjoy the water and sunshine.

Safety Precautions: While SUP is generally considered safe, it's essential to wear a PFD and use sunscreen for sun protection. Be mindful of tides, currents, and weather conditions, and always practice safe paddling.

Guided Tours: If you're new to paddleboarding or want a guided experience, many outfitters offer guided SUP tours. These tours often include additional insights into the local environment and wildlife.

Rentals and Classes: Be sure to check with local water sports rental shops for rental availability, prices, and any classes or tours they may offer.

Stand-up paddleboarding on the Gulf of Mexico provides a refreshing and active way to connect with the natural beauty of the coast. It's an accessible and enjoyable activity for people of various skill levels, whether you're an experienced paddleboarder or trying it for the first time. Enjoy the sunshine, the sea breeze, and the serenity of the Gulf while exploring the St. Petersburg area from a different perspective.

33.Go fishing off the St. Petersburg Pier.

Fishing off the St. Petersburg Pier is a popular activity that allows you to enjoy the Gulf of Mexico's rich marine life and reel in a variety of fish species. Here's what you can expect when you go fishing at the St. Petersburg Pier:

Pier Amenities: The St. Petersburg Pier provides fishing amenities, including designated fishing areas, cleaning stations for fish, and benches for anglers to relax and enjoy the experience.

Fishing Gear: You can bring your own fishing gear, or you may find tackle shops or rental options nearby where you can acquire the necessary equipment, such as fishing rods, reels, and bait.

Saltwater Species: Fishing off the pier offers the opportunity to catch a variety of saltwater species. Common catches include snook, redfish, trout, sheepshead, snapper, and various types of mackerel.

Fishing Techniques: The choice of fishing techniques varies, and anglers often use live or frozen bait, lures, and even fly-fishing methods, depending on the targeted species and conditions.

Local Regulations: Make sure to familiarize yourself with local fishing regulations, including size and bag limits for specific species, as well as catch-and-release guidelines.

Fishing Charters: If you're new to fishing or prefer a guided experience, you can consider booking a fishing charter from the pier, with experienced captains who know the best spots to catch fish.

Enjoying the Scenery: While fishing, take in the beautiful views of the Gulf of Mexico and the surrounding waterfront. The pier is known for its stunning sunsets, offering a serene backdrop to your fishing adventure.

Sun Protection: Since you'll be spending time in the Florida sun, it's essential to use sunscreen, wear a hat, and stay hydrated to protect yourself from the elements.

Pier Facilities: The St. Petersburg Pier typically offers facilities like restrooms, food vendors, and souvenir shops, ensuring a comfortable and convenient fishing experience.

Check the Local Conditions: Before your fishing trip, check local weather conditions, tides, and fishing reports to optimize your chances of a successful catch.

Fishing off the St. Petersburg Pier is a relaxing and enjoyable activity, whether you're an experienced angler or new to the sport. It's an excellent way to connect with the region's marine life, appreciate the natural surroundings, and possibly bring home a delicious catch for dinner. Don't forget to follow local fishing guidelines and respect the marine environment for a sustainable and enjoyable fishing experience.

34.Experience the annual Firestone Grand Prix.

Experiencing the annual Firestone Grand Prix in St. Petersburg, Florida, is a thrilling motorsports event that offers high-speed racing, entertainment, and a festive atmosphere. Here's what you can expect when you attend the Firestone Grand Prix:

IndyCar Racing: The Firestone Grand Prix is part of the NTT IndyCar Series, one of the premier open-wheel racing series in the United States. You'll witness world-class drivers competing on a challenging street circuit.

Street Circuit: The race takes place on a temporary street circuit in downtown St. Petersburg. The track layout is known for its technical challenges and tight turns, making for exciting racing.

Support Races: In addition to the IndyCar race, the event often features support races from various racing series, such as Indy Lights and sports car championships, providing a full weekend of motorsports action.

Entertainment: The Firestone Grand Prix typically offers a range of entertainment options, including live music, food vendors, interactive exhibits, and activities for all ages.

Fan Zone: Many events have a designated fan zone where you can meet drivers, get autographs, and explore interactive displays related to motorsports.

Paddock Access: Some ticket options may provide access to the paddock, allowing you to get up close to the teams, cars, and mechanics for a behind-the-scenes experience.

Spectacular Views: The track offers various vantage points for spectators to watch the races, including grandstands, bleachers, and viewing areas along the waterfront, which provide scenic views of the bay.

Family-Friendly: The event is family-friendly, and there are often kid zones and family activities to keep children entertained.

Community Engagement: The Firestone Grand Prix engages with the local community through various outreach initiatives, charities, and educational programs.

Check the Schedule: Be sure to check the event's schedule, ticket availability, and any special experiences or packages that may be available, such as VIP hospitality options.

Attending the Firestone Grand Prix is an opportunity to witness high-speed racing up close, enjoy entertainment, and immerse yourself in the excitement of motorsports. Whether you're a racing enthusiast, a sports fan, or someone looking for a thrilling and action-packed event, the Firestone Grand Prix provides a memorable experience in the heart of St. Petersburg, Florida.

35.Join a guided kayaking tour.

Joining a guided kayaking tour in St. Petersburg, Florida, is an excellent way to explore the area's natural beauty, waterways, and wildlife. Here's what you can expect when you take part in a guided kayaking tour:

Tour Guides: Knowledgeable and experienced guides lead the tours. They often provide safety instructions, paddling tips, and insights into the local environment.

Travel to St. Petersburg Florida

Scenic Routes: Guided kayaking tours typically take you through picturesque waterways, such as coastal mangroves, estuaries, and wildlife habitats. You'll have the opportunity to enjoy the natural beauty of the area.

Wildlife Viewing: Florida's waterways are home to a diverse range of wildlife. During the tour, you may spot dolphins, manatees, various bird species, and even small fish swimming beneath your kayak.

Equipment Provided: Most guided tours include all necessary kayaking equipment, including kayaks, paddles, life jackets, and sometimes waterproof bags for personal items.

Paddling Instruction: If you're new to kayaking, guides often provide paddling instruction and safety guidelines to ensure a safe and enjoyable experience.

Educational Insights: Guides may share information about the local ecosystem, including details about the plants, animals, and habitats you encounter during the tour.

Group Experience: Kayaking tours are usually conducted in small groups, creating a social and enjoyable atmosphere for participants.

Photography Opportunities: The scenic beauty and wildlife encounters provide excellent opportunities for photography, so be sure to bring a waterproof camera or smartphone to capture the moments.

Sun Protection: Since you'll be out on the water, it's important to apply sunscreen, wear a hat, and bring sunglasses to protect yourself from the sun.

Check Availability: Be sure to check with local tour operators for available tours, schedules, and any age or skill-level requirements.

Guided kayaking tours in St. Petersburg offer a unique and serene way to experience the natural beauty of the area and connect with the local environment. Whether you're a nature enthusiast, an outdoor adventurer, or someone seeking a peaceful and educational experience, these tours provide an enriching and memorable way to explore the coastal waterways of Florida.

36.Explore local beaches: St. Pete Beach, Pass-a-Grille Beach, Treasure Island

Exploring the local beaches of St. Petersburg, Florida, including St. Pete Beach, Pass-a-Grille Beach, and Treasure Island, is a fantastic way to enjoy the sun, sand, and the stunning Gulf of Mexico. Here's what you can expect when you visit these beautiful beaches:

St. Pete Beach:

White Sand: St. Pete Beach is known for its wide stretches of soft, white sand, perfect for sunbathing and building sandcastles.
Swimming: The calm, clear waters of the Gulf are ideal for swimming and wading.
Beachfront Activities: You'll find beachfront bars, restaurants, and water sports rentals along the coastline, offering options for dining and entertainment.
Pass-a-Grille Beach:

Historic Charm: Pass-a-Grille Beach is a historic and quaint community with a charming atmosphere. It offers a quieter and more relaxed beach experience.
Sunsets: The area is known for its stunning sunsets, and many visitors gather in the evening to watch the sun go down over the Gulf.
Treasure Island:

Family-Friendly: Treasure Island is family-friendly and offers a wide range of amenities, including picnic areas, playgrounds, and beachfront hotels.
John's Pass: Nearby John's Pass Village and Boardwalk provide shopping, dining, and entertainment options.
Water Sports: All three beaches offer opportunities for various water sports activities, such as parasailing, jet skiing, paddleboarding, and more. Rental shops are usually available for equipment.

Fishing: Anglers can enjoy fishing from the shores, piers, or charters offered in the area. Pass-a-Grille Beach and Treasure Island have fishing piers.

Dining: You'll find numerous beachfront and waterfront restaurants and bars, allowing you to enjoy delicious meals with ocean views.

Shelling: Beachcombers can search for seashells along the shore, particularly in the early morning or during low tide.

Events: Check local event calendars for beach events, festivals, and concerts that may be happening during your visit.

Waterfront Parks: Some areas near these beaches have waterfront parks with facilities, making them great spots for family outings.

Sun Protection: Remember to use sunscreen, wear a hat, and stay hydrated to protect yourself from the sun.

Exploring St. Pete Beach, Pass-a-Grille Beach, and Treasure Island provides a variety of beach experiences, from vibrant and lively to historic and tranquil. Whether you're looking for water sports, family fun, or a relaxing day in the sun, these local beaches offer something for everyone. Enjoy the beautiful Gulf Coast and the warm Florida sunshine during your visit.

37.Relax on the pristine Fort De Soto Beach.

Relaxing on the pristine Fort De Soto Beach is a perfect way to enjoy the natural beauty of the St. Petersburg area. Here's what you can expect when you visit Fort De Soto Beach:

Powdery White Sand: Fort De Soto Beach is known for its soft, powdery white sand that's perfect for lounging, making sandcastles, or taking a leisurely walk along the shore.

Crystal-Clear Waters: The Gulf of Mexico's clear, calm waters are ideal for swimming and wading, especially for families with young children.

Picnicking and Shelling: The beach offers picnic shelters and tables, as well as opportunities for shelling along the shore.

Kayaking and Canoeing: Fort De Soto Park has kayaking and canoeing trails, allowing you to explore the nearby mangroves and bay areas.

Fishing: Anglers can try their luck from the fishing pier, and there are also opportunities for surf fishing.

Wildlife Viewing: The park is home to various wildlife species, and you might spot birds, dolphins, and other animals while enjoying the beach.

Dog-Friendly Areas: Fort De Soto Park includes a dog beach where pets are allowed to run and play off-leash in designated areas.

Camping: The park features a campground for those who want to experience beachfront camping. Be sure to check availability and make reservations in advance.

Bicycling and Hiking: You can explore the park's trails and scenic areas by bicycle or on foot.

Historical Landmarks: The park also includes historic remnants from the Spanish-American War, providing an opportunity for a bit of history.

Eco-Friendly: Fort De Soto Park is known for its commitment to environmental conservation and sustainability.

Sun Protection: As with any beach visit, it's essential to use sunscreen, wear a hat, and stay hydrated to protect yourself from the sun.

Fort De Soto Beach is a serene and unspoiled gem along the Gulf Coast, offering a peaceful and pristine environment for beachgoers. Whether you're looking for a tranquil day by the sea, outdoor activities, or a place to connect with nature, Fort De Soto Beach is a beautiful destination to relax and unwind in the St. Petersburg area.

38. Go shelling at Shell Key Preserve.

Visiting Shell Key Preserve near St. Petersburg, Florida, is an excellent choice for shelling enthusiasts and nature lovers. Here's what you can expect when you go shelling at Shell Key Preserve:

Unspoiled Natural Beauty: Shell Key Preserve is an undeveloped barrier island located in the Gulf of Mexico. It is known for its pristine and unspoiled natural beauty, making it a haven for shelling and wildlife.

Access: Access to Shell Key Preserve is typically by boat. You can take a water taxi or join guided tours offered by local operators, which often include shelling excursions.

Travel to St. Petersburg Florida

Shelling Paradise: The preserve is renowned for its abundance of seashells, including conch shells, sand dollars, whelks, and various other shells. Shelling opportunities can be particularly good after storms or during low tide.

Wildlife Viewing: Shell Key Preserve is a protected habitat for various bird species, such as shorebirds and seabirds. You may also spot dolphins, manatees, and other marine life in the surrounding waters.

Picnicking: The island provides picnic areas, so you can enjoy a beachfront picnic after a successful shelling adventure.

Lighthouse: The southern end of the preserve is home to the historic Egmont Key Lighthouse, which adds a touch of history to your visit.

Environmental Conservation: As a protected area, Shell Key Preserve has a strong emphasis on environmental conservation and respecting the natural ecosystem.

Beachcombing Tips: When shelling, be sure to bring a mesh bag or bucket to collect your treasures. It's important to follow ethical beachcombing guidelines, such as not taking live shells and respecting the environment.

Tide and Weather: Shelling conditions can be influenced by tides and weather, so it's a good idea to check the tides and weather forecast before your visit.

Leave No Trace: In the spirit of conservation, make sure to clean up any trash and leave the preserve as pristine as you found it.

Visiting Shell Key Preserve is a unique and rewarding experience for beachcombers and nature enthusiasts. You can immerse yourself in the natural beauty of a remote and unspoiled island, discover beautiful seashells, and enjoy the serenity of a pristine coastal environment. Don't forget to capture the moment and take home some of the treasures you find as souvenirs of your shelling adventure.

39.Experience parasailing on the Gulf of Mexico.

Experiencing parasailing on the Gulf of Mexico is an exhilarating and unforgettable adventure. Here's what you can expect when you go parasailing in the St. Petersburg area:

Safety Briefing: Before your parasailing adventure, you'll typically receive a safety briefing from trained guides. They will provide instructions on how to wear your safety harness and what to expect during the experience.

Equipment: You'll be provided with a harness and a parachute-like sail, often called a parasail, that's attached to the back of a boat. The boat is specially designed for parasailing and has a platform where you'll take off and land.

Takeoff: You'll be securely attached to the parasail, and as the boat accelerates, you'll gradually ascend into the air. The feeling of taking off and soaring above the water is both exhilarating and peaceful.

Spectacular Views: As you ascend, you'll enjoy breathtaking views of the Gulf of Mexico, the coastline, and the surrounding area. Parasailing provides a unique perspective of the water and landscape.

Altitude: The altitude you'll reach during your parasailing experience can vary, but it's often around 300 to 500 feet above the water.

Tandem and Triple Rides: Many parasailing operators offer the option to parasail with a partner or in a group, allowing you to share the experience with friends or family.

Optional Dips: Some operators offer the chance to cool off by dipping your feet in the water while parasailing. It's a refreshing way to enhance your adventure.

Photos and Videos: Many operators offer the option to purchase photos or videos of your parasailing experience, so you can relive the excitement and share it with others.

Duration: Parasailing rides typically last around 10 to 15 minutes, but some operators offer longer rides.

Safety: Parasailing operators follow strict safety protocols, and the equipment is regularly inspected to ensure a safe and enjoyable experience.

Weather Conditions: Parasailing is dependent on weather conditions, so it's important to check the weather forecast before your adventure to ensure safe and suitable conditions for parasailing.

Age and Weight Restrictions: Parasailing operators may have age and weight restrictions, so it's advisable to check with the operator in advance.

Parasailing on the Gulf of Mexico is a thrilling way to enjoy the stunning coastal scenery, experience the sensation of flight, and create lasting memories. Whether you're an adventure seeker or looking for a unique way to appreciate the beauty of the Gulf, parasailing is an exciting and picturesque activity in the St. Petersburg area.

40. Take a dolphin-watching tour.

Taking a dolphin-watching tour in the St. Petersburg area is a delightful way to see these intelligent and playful marine mammals in their natural habitat. Here's what you can expect when you embark on a dolphin-watching tour:

Experienced Guides: Dolphin-watching tours are led by experienced and knowledgeable guides who are familiar with the local waters and the behavior of dolphins.

Boat Excursion: Most tours are conducted on boats, with various options available, including small group tours, private charters, and eco-friendly boat tours.

Scenic Routes: Tours typically follow scenic routes along the Gulf of Mexico, through coastal areas, and around islands known for dolphin activity.

Dolphin Behavior: Guides will share insights into dolphin behavior, including how to identify different species and what to look for when observing their movements and interactions.

Wildlife Viewing: While the main focus is on dolphins, you may also spot other marine life, such as manatees, sea turtles, and various bird species.

Interactive Experience: Depending on the tour, you may have opportunities to see dolphins up close, watch them jump and play, and even hear them communicate with each other.

Safety Measures: Tours prioritize the safety and well-being of the dolphins, with guidelines in place to ensure a respectful and responsible wildlife-watching experience.

Educational Insights: In addition to dolphin watching, you may learn about the local marine ecosystem, conservation efforts, and the significance of protecting these creatures and their habitat.

Photography Opportunities: Be sure to bring a camera or smartphone to capture the moments and create lasting memories of your dolphin-watching experience.

Check Availability: Make reservations in advance, especially during peak tourist seasons, to secure your spot on a dolphin-watching tour.

Dolphin-watching tours are not only a fun and memorable experience but also an opportunity to connect with nature and appreciate the beauty of the Gulf Coast. Whether you're a wildlife enthusiast, a family looking for an educational outing, or simply someone who enjoys the wonder of the sea, a dolphin-watching tour in the St. Petersburg area provides a rewarding and enchanting adventure.

41.Enjoy sunset cruises.

Enjoying a sunset cruise in the St. Petersburg area is a romantic and serene way to appreciate the breathtaking beauty of the Gulf of Mexico as the sun sets on the horizon. Here's what you can expect when you take a sunset cruise:

Scenic Setting: Sunset cruises typically take place on the calm and clear waters of the Gulf of Mexico, offering spectacular views of the coastline, islands, and the setting sun.

Choice of Vessels: Sunset cruises are offered on a variety of vessels, including sailboats, catamarans, and traditional motorized boats. You can choose the type of vessel that best suits your preferences.

Romantic Atmosphere: Sunset cruises are often chosen for romantic outings, making them popular for couples celebrating special occasions or simply looking for a romantic experience.

Sunset Views: You'll have the opportunity to witness the stunning transformation of the sky as the sun sets, casting warm and vibrant colors across the water.

Dolphin Sightings: Depending on the cruise, you may also have the chance to spot dolphins and other marine life as they become more active during the twilight hours.

Refreshments: Many sunset cruises offer light refreshments and beverages, which can enhance the experience as you relax and enjoy the sunset.

Live Music: Some cruises feature live music, adding to the ambiance and creating a delightful and entertaining atmosphere.

Photography: Don't forget to bring a camera or smartphone to capture the beauty of the sunset and create lasting memories.

Duration: Sunset cruises typically last for a couple of hours, allowing you to fully savor the sunset and the tranquil waters.

Reservations: It's a good idea to make reservations in advance, especially during the peak tourist season, to ensure you secure a spot on the cruise.

Sunset cruises are a popular and cherished activity in the St. Petersburg area, offering a peaceful and picturesque way to end the day. Whether you're celebrating a special occasion, looking for a romantic experience, or simply wanting to appreciate the natural beauty of the Gulf, a sunset cruise provides a serene and memorable way to connect with the coastal environment.

42. Try jet skiing or wave-running.

Trying jet skiing or wave-running in the St. Petersburg area is a thrilling water adventure that allows you to experience the Gulf of Mexico's excitement and beauty. Here's what you can expect when you take to the water on a jet ski or wave runner:

Rental Options: Various rental shops and water sports operators in the area offer jet ski and wave runner rentals. You can choose from different rental durations, including hourly or daily options.

Safety Instructions: Before you embark on your jet ski adventure, you'll receive safety instructions and guidelines from experienced staff. It's important to follow these instructions for a safe and enjoyable ride.

Life Jackets: You'll be provided with life jackets, which are essential for safety while on the water.

Watercraft Operation: Jet skis and wave runners are easy to operate, with throttle and steering controls. Staff will typically provide basic training on how to control and maneuver the watercraft.

Scenic Routes: You'll have the freedom to explore the Gulf of Mexico at your own pace. Popular routes include cruising along the coastline, venturing to nearby islands, and enjoying scenic views of the shoreline.

Thrilling Speed: Jet skis and wave runners are known for their speed and agility. You can race across the water, make sharp turns, and experience an adrenaline rush.

Wildlife Viewing: Keep an eye out for marine life, such as dolphins, manatees, and various bird species that may be visible as you zip across the water.

Group Rides: You can ride solo or in tandem with a partner, making it a great option for couples, friends, or family members looking for a shared adventure.

Photography: Bring a waterproof camera or smartphone to capture the excitement and beautiful coastal scenery as you ride.

Safety Precautions: Be sure to follow safety guidelines, including wearing a life jacket, practicing responsible watercraft operation, and respecting wildlife and other water users.

Jet skiing and wave running in the St. Petersburg area offer a thrilling and scenic way to enjoy the Gulf of Mexico. Whether you're an adventure seeker, a water sports enthusiast, or someone simply looking for a fun and active day on the water, jet skiing and wave running provide an exciting and memorable experience along the beautiful Florida coast.

43. Take a scenic boat tour of the area.

Taking a scenic boat tour of the St. Petersburg area is a relaxing and picturesque way to explore the coastal beauty and natural wonders of the region. Here's what you can expect when you embark on a scenic boat tour:

Variety of Tours: There are different types of boat tours to choose from, including sightseeing tours, eco-tours, wildlife tours, and historical tours. You can select the one that aligns with your interests.

Experienced Guides: Knowledgeable guides provide insights into the local environment, wildlife, history, and points of interest along the tour route.

Scenic Routes: Boat tours often follow scenic routes through coastal areas, islands, and waterways, offering picturesque views of the Gulf of Mexico and the surrounding landscape.

Wildlife Viewing: Depending on the tour, you may have the opportunity to spot wildlife, such as dolphins, manatees, sea turtles, and various bird species.

Eco-Friendly Tours: Some operators offer eco-friendly tours that focus on the area's ecology and conservation efforts, providing an educational and environmentally responsible experience.

Historical Insights: Historical boat tours may include visits to historical landmarks or offer information about the area's cultural and maritime history.

Sunset Tours: Sunset boat tours provide a romantic and serene experience as you watch the sun set over the Gulf of Mexico.

Refreshments: Some tours offer light refreshments and beverages, allowing you to relax and enjoy the journey.

Photography: Be sure to bring a camera or smartphone to capture the scenic beauty and wildlife sightings during the tour.

Duration: Boat tours vary in duration, so you can choose the one that fits your schedule and preferences.

Check Availability: Reservations are recommended, especially during peak tourist seasons, to secure your spot on the boat tour.

Scenic boat tours in the St. Petersburg area offer a leisurely and enjoyable way to connect with the coastal environment and appreciate the natural beauty of the Gulf Coast. Whether you're interested in wildlife, history, or simply a peaceful day on the water, a boat tour provides a captivating and memorable experience.

44.Go deep-sea fishing in the Gulf.

Going deep-sea fishing in the Gulf of Mexico near St. Petersburg is an exciting and adventurous activity for anglers and fishing enthusiasts. Here's what you can expect when you embark on a deep-sea fishing excursion:

Charter Options: There are several charter fishing companies in the St. Petersburg area that offer deep-sea fishing excursions. You can choose from a variety of charters, including private charters or shared trips.

Experienced Crew: Most deep-sea fishing charters are led by experienced captains and crews who are knowledgeable about the best fishing spots, techniques, and local marine life.

Types of Fish: The Gulf of Mexico offers diverse fishing opportunities. Common catches during deep-sea fishing excursions include grouper, snapper, kingfish, amberjack, and even larger species like sharks and barracuda.

Equipment Provided: Charters typically provide all the necessary fishing equipment, including fishing rods, reels, bait, tackle, and fishing licenses.

Fishing Techniques: You'll have the chance to try different fishing techniques, such as bottom fishing, trolling, and live bait fishing, depending on the targeted species and conditions.

Scenic Adventure: Deep-sea fishing allows you to venture far out into the Gulf, providing an adventurous and scenic experience as you cruise over deep waters.

Wildlife Encounters: While fishing, you might also have opportunities to spot dolphins, sea turtles, and various bird species in their natural habitat.

Full-Day or Half-Day: Deep-sea fishing charters offer options for both full-day and half-day trips, so you can select the one that suits your schedule and preferences.

Sun Protection: Be sure to use sunscreen, wear a hat, and stay hydrated to protect yourself from the sun during your fishing adventure.

Catch and Release: Some charters promote catch-and-release practices to conserve fish populations, while others allow you to keep your catch for consumption.

Fishing Records: The Gulf of Mexico is known for record-sized catches, so you might even have the opportunity to reel in a personal best.

Booking in Advance: To secure your spot on a deep-sea fishing charter, it's advisable to book your trip in advance, especially during busy fishing seasons.

Deep-sea fishing in the Gulf of Mexico is a thrilling and rewarding experience for both seasoned anglers and those new to fishing. It's an opportunity to test your skills, enjoy the open water, and potentially bring home a memorable catch. Whether you're looking for a challenging adventure or a relaxing day on the water, deep-sea fishing in the St. Petersburg area offers a diverse and exciting fishing experience.

45.Explore the vibrant downtown waterfront.

Exploring the vibrant downtown waterfront of St. Petersburg, Florida, is a delightful way to soak in the city's culture, art, and scenic beauty. Here's what you can expect when you visit this dynamic area:

Scenic Walks: The downtown waterfront features scenic walkways along the waterfront, providing breathtaking views of Tampa Bay and the city skyline.

Parks and Green Spaces: The area boasts several parks, including North Straub Park and South Straub Park, where you can relax, have a picnic, or enjoy open spaces for recreational activities.

Waterfront Dining: You'll find numerous waterfront restaurants and cafes offering a diverse range of cuisines. Enjoy a meal while overlooking the water.

Shopping: Explore local boutiques and shops along Beach Drive and nearby streets for unique clothing, gifts, and art.

Museums and Galleries: The downtown waterfront is home to several museums and galleries, including the Salvador Dali Museum, the Museum of Fine Arts, and various contemporary art galleries.

Cultural Events: Check the local event calendar for cultural and artistic events, including outdoor concerts, art shows, and festivals.

Vinoy Park: This historic park often hosts outdoor events and is a beautiful spot to take a leisurely stroll or have a picnic.

Marina Activities: The downtown marina offers opportunities for boating, fishing, and watching boats and yachts go by.

Sundial St. Pete: This shopping and dining complex features a variety of restaurants, shops, and entertainment options.

Vinoy Hotel: The historic Vinoy Hotel, a Mediterranean Revival-style resort, adds a touch of grandeur to the waterfront area.

Sundial Fountain: The Sundial St. Pete area often includes a lively fountain where children can play and cool off during the warmer months.

Bicycle Rentals: You can rent bicycles to explore the waterfront area and nearby neighborhoods, including the beautiful Old Northeast district.

Public Art: The waterfront is adorned with public art installations and sculptures, making it an outdoor art gallery.

Festivals: Depending on the time of year, you may be able to enjoy local festivals, food and wine events, and holiday celebrations along the waterfront.

Sunsets: The downtown waterfront is famous for its stunning sunsets. Join the locals and visitors who gather to watch the sun dip below the horizon.

Exploring the downtown waterfront of St. Petersburg is a multi-faceted experience, offering a mix of culture, recreation, and natural beauty. Whether you're interested in art, dining, outdoor activities, or simply a leisurely stroll along the water, the waterfront area provides a vibrant and engaging atmosphere for visitors and residents alike.

46.Enjoy a day at North Straub Park.

Spending a day at North Straub Park in St. Petersburg is a relaxing and enjoyable way to connect with nature, have a picnic, and take in the scenic surroundings. Here's what you can expect when you visit North Straub Park:

Green Oasis: North Straub Park is a lush and well-maintained green space located along the downtown waterfront. It's an urban oasis where you can escape the city's hustle and bustle.

Picnicking: The park provides picnic tables, benches, and open spaces, making it an ideal spot for a picnic with family or friends. Pack a picnic basket and enjoy a meal surrounded by nature.

Waterfront Views: The park offers beautiful waterfront views of Tampa Bay and is known for its stunning sunsets. It's a popular place to watch the sun go down.

Walking Paths: There are paved walking paths that wind through the park, allowing for leisurely strolls and a bit of exercise. It's a pleasant place for a morning jog or an evening walk.

Public Art: North Straub Park features public art installations and sculptures, adding an artistic touch to the natural surroundings.

Relaxation: Benches and shaded areas are scattered throughout the park, offering plenty of places to relax, read a book, or simply unwind.

Events and Activities: The park occasionally hosts events, festivals, and gatherings, so check the local event calendar for any happenings during your visit.

Waterfront Dining: Nearby restaurants and cafes offer the opportunity to enjoy a meal or a refreshing beverage with waterfront views.

Playground: The park includes a playground, making it a family-friendly destination where kids can have fun.

Birdwatching: Bird enthusiasts may spot various bird species along the waterfront, including pelicans and herons.

Scenic Photography: North Straub Park is a great place for photography, especially during sunset when the sky is painted with vibrant colors.

Pets: Leashed dogs are allowed in the park, providing an opportunity to enjoy the outdoors with your furry friends.

North Straub Park is a serene and inviting green space where you can unwind, enjoy nature, and take in the scenic waterfront views. Whether you're looking for a quiet day of relaxation, a family outing, or a picturesque place to enjoy a meal, this park provides a tranquil and welcoming setting in the heart of St. Petersburg.

47. Visit Vinoy Park for picnics and events.

Visiting Vinoy Park in St. Petersburg, Florida, is a wonderful way to enjoy a scenic and historic park with a range of activities and events. Here's what you can expect when you visit Vinoy Park:

Picnics: Vinoy Park is an excellent spot for picnics and outdoor dining. You can bring a picnic basket, lay out a blanket, and enjoy a meal with family or friends in a picturesque setting.

Waterfront Views: The park is located along the waterfront, offering stunning views of Tampa Bay, the marina, and the surrounding area. It's a prime location to watch the sunset over the bay.

Recreational Activities: Vinoy Park features open spaces for recreational activities like frisbee, kite flying, or simply relaxing in the shade. You'll find plenty of room for outdoor fun.

Events and Festivals: The park hosts a variety of events and festivals throughout the year, including concerts, food and wine festivals, art shows, and cultural celebrations. Be sure to check the local event calendar for any happenings during your visit.

Vinoy Hotel: The historic Vinoy Hotel, located adjacent to the park, is an architectural gem and a notable landmark in the area. You can explore the hotel's grounds and enjoy its elegance.

Walking and Jogging: There are paved walking paths in the park, making it a great place for a morning jog or a leisurely stroll.

Public Art: Vinoy Park is adorned with public art installations and sculptures, creating an artistic and engaging atmosphere.

Sunbathing and Relaxation: The park offers plenty of benches, shaded areas, and grassy spots where you can relax and enjoy the tranquil surroundings.

Dining Options: Nearby restaurants and cafes provide an opportunity to enjoy a meal or a beverage with waterfront views.

Waterfront Access: The park has direct access to the waterfront, making it a great place for water activities like kayaking, paddleboarding, and boat watching.

Playground: Vinoy Park includes a playground, making it family-friendly and an ideal place for children to play.

Pets: Leashed dogs are allowed in the park, so you can enjoy the outdoors with your four-legged companions.

Vinoy Park is a versatile and welcoming destination, offering a blend of natural beauty, historical charm, and cultural vibrancy. Whether you're interested in outdoor recreation, enjoying a picnic, attending an event, or simply savoring the beauty of the waterfront, Vinoy Park provides a delightful and scenic experience in St. Petersburg.

48.Relax in South Straub Park.

Relaxing in South Straub Park in St. Petersburg, Florida, is a tranquil and peaceful way to enjoy green spaces, waterfront views, and the gentle ambiance of the downtown area. Here's what you can expect when you visit South Straub Park:

Serene Environment: South Straub Park is a well-maintained urban green space that offers a peaceful escape from the city's hustle and bustle.

Waterfront Location: The park is situated along the waterfront, providing lovely views of Tampa Bay and the iconic St. Petersburg Pier.

Picnicking: The park includes picnic tables and shaded areas, making it an ideal spot for a relaxing picnic with family or friends.

Scenic Walks: Paved walkways meander through the park, allowing for leisurely strolls or brisk walks. The paths provide scenic views of the waterfront and nearby landmarks.

Relaxation: Benches are scattered throughout the park, offering places to sit and enjoy the serene surroundings, read a book, or simply unwind.

Public Art: South Straub Park features public art installations and sculptures, contributing to the park's artistic and engaging atmosphere.

Fountain and Water Features: The park often includes fountains and water features, adding to the park's soothing ambiance and creating opportunities for playful enjoyment.

Events and Festivals: The park occasionally hosts events, festivals, and gatherings. Check the local event calendar for any happenings during your visit.

Sunsets: South Straub Park is a popular spot to watch the sun set over Tampa Bay. Many locals and visitors gather here to witness the stunning evening views.

Waterfront Dining: Nearby restaurants and cafes offer the opportunity to enjoy a meal or a refreshing beverage with waterfront views.

Sculpture Garden: The park's sculpture garden showcases a rotating collection of artworks, making it a must-visit for art enthusiasts.

Pet-Friendly: Leashed dogs are welcome in the park, allowing you to enjoy the outdoors with your canine companions.

South Straub Park is a charming and tranquil destination where you can immerse yourself in the natural beauty of the waterfront, have a leisurely picnic, or simply unwind in a serene environment. Whether you're looking for a peaceful day of relaxation, a scenic spot for outdoor activities, or a place to enjoy artistic displays, South Straub Park provides a calming and inviting atmosphere in the heart of downtown St. Petersburg.

49.Go to Flora Wylie Park for its playground.

Flora Wylie Park in St. Petersburg, Florida, is a family-friendly destination known for its playground and recreational amenities. Here's what you can expect when you visit Flora Wylie Park:

Playground: The park is home to a playground designed for children to enjoy. It features swings, slides, climbing structures, and other play equipment that provides a fun and safe environment for kids.

Picnic Facilities: Flora Wylie Park offers picnic tables and shelters where you can have a picnic lunch or snacks with your family.

Open Spaces: The park has open green spaces where kids can run and play, and families can engage in recreational activities like frisbee or catch.

Shaded Areas: Shaded areas are available to provide relief from the sun during hot Florida days. They're perfect for parents and caregivers to relax while keeping an eye on their children.

Basketball Court: The park includes a basketball court, making it a great spot for friendly games or shooting some hoops.

Community Gatherings: Flora Wylie Park is often used for community gatherings, events, and celebrations. Check the local event calendar for any happenings during your visit.

Walking Paths: Paved paths wind through the park, offering opportunities for leisurely walks and strolls.

Restrooms: The park typically provides restroom facilities for visitors' convenience.

Pet-Friendly: Leashed dogs are welcome in the park, making it a place where families can bring their four-legged friends.

Accessibility: The park is generally designed to be accessible to people with disabilities, ensuring that everyone can enjoy its amenities.

Flora Wylie Park is a great place for families and children to have a day of outdoor fun and play. Whether you're looking for a spot to let your kids burn off some energy, enjoy a picnic, or engage in recreational activities, this park provides a welcoming and enjoyable setting in St. Petersburg.

50.Discover the nature trails of Coquina Key Park.

Exploring the nature trails of Coquina Key Park in St. Petersburg is a wonderful way to connect with the natural beauty of the area and enjoy outdoor activities. Here's what you can expect when you visit Coquina Key Park:

Tranquil Environment: Coquina Key Park offers a serene and natural environment where you can escape the urban hustle and bustle and immerse yourself in nature.

Nature Trails: The park features nature trails that wind through wooded areas, salt marshes, and coastal habitats. These trails provide opportunities for hiking, walking, and birdwatching.

Scenic Views: As you explore the trails, you'll encounter scenic views of the surrounding landscape, including glimpses of Tampa Bay and local flora and fauna.

Wildlife Observation: The park is home to various wildlife, including birds, reptiles, and possibly small mammals. It's an excellent spot for birdwatching and wildlife observation.

Boardwalks: Some sections of the trails include boardwalks that take you through marshy areas, providing a unique perspective of the coastal ecosystem.

Educational Signage: Along the trails, you may find educational signage that offers information about the park's ecology, wildlife, and environmental conservation efforts.

Picnic Facilities: Coquina Key Park provides picnic tables and areas where you can enjoy a meal surrounded by the natural beauty of the park.

Fishing Opportunities: The park has a fishing pier where you can cast a line and try your luck at catching local fish.

Canoe and Kayak Launch: If you have your own canoe or kayak, there is a launch area at the park, allowing you to explore the waterways surrounding the park.

Restrooms: Restroom facilities are typically available for visitors' convenience.

Dog-Friendly: Leashed dogs are welcome in the park, so you can enjoy the trails with your furry companions.

Coquina Key Park offers a tranquil and scenic setting for those who appreciate the outdoors, nature, and wildlife. Whether you're interested in hiking, birdwatching, or simply a peaceful walk in a natural environment, the nature trails of Coquina Key Park provide a welcoming and engaging experience in St. Petersburg.

51.Enjoy a game of beach volleyball.

Playing beach volleyball in the St. Petersburg area is a fun and active way to enjoy the beautiful beaches and coastal atmosphere. Here's what you can expect when you indulge in a game of beach volleyball:

Sandy Beaches: The St. Petersburg area boasts several sandy beaches along the Gulf of Mexico, providing the ideal setting for beach volleyball.

Public Volleyball Nets: Many beaches offer public volleyball nets or courts, where you can play with friends, join a pickup game, or even participate in beach volleyball tournaments if available.

Scenic Backdrop: While playing, you'll have the stunning backdrop of the Gulf of Mexico and the beach, creating a picturesque setting for your games.

Relaxed Atmosphere: Beach volleyball is a popular recreational activity in the area, and the vibe is typically laid-back and welcoming. It's an excellent way to socialize and have fun.

Family-Friendly: Beach volleyball is a family-friendly activity, so it's a great way to spend quality time with loved ones and get some exercise.

Tournaments: Depending on the season, you might come across organized beach volleyball tournaments and events if you're looking for a more competitive experience.

Sun and Fun: Florida's sunny weather and warm temperatures make beach volleyball an enjoyable outdoor activity year-round.

Beach Amenities: Many beaches offer amenities such as restrooms, picnic areas, and nearby eateries where you can grab refreshments.

Sun Protection: Don't forget to apply sunscreen, wear a hat, and stay hydrated to protect yourself from the sun's rays during your beach volleyball games.

Accessibility: Beach volleyball is an accessible activity for people of various skill levels, making it suitable for beginners and experienced players alike.

Beach volleyball is a popular and enjoyable way to soak up the sun, get active, and have a great time with friends and fellow beachgoers in the St. Petersburg area. Whether you're seeking friendly matches, a competitive challenge, or a casual game by the sea, the local beaches provide the perfect backdrop for beach volleyball fun.

52.Take a morning yoga class on the beach.

Taking a morning yoga class on the beach in the St. Petersburg area is a rejuvenating and peaceful way to start your day while connecting with nature. Here's what you can expect when you participate in a beach yoga class:

Scenic Setting: Yoga classes on the beach are typically held on the sandy shores of the Gulf of Mexico, providing a stunning backdrop of the sea, the horizon, and the natural beauty of the coast.

Fresh Air: Practicing yoga by the sea allows you to breathe in the fresh ocean air, which can enhance your yoga experience and promote relaxation.

Beach Atmosphere: The beach setting offers a serene and calming atmosphere, making it an ideal place to find inner peace and balance.

Travel to St. Petersburg Florida

Certified Instructors: Classes are usually led by certified yoga instructors who can guide you through a yoga session suitable for all levels, from beginners to experienced yogis.

Morning Sun: Morning classes offer the advantage of practicing yoga in the gentle morning sun, which can be invigorating and energizing.

Sound of the Waves: The soothing sound of the waves serves as a natural soundtrack to your yoga practice, enhancing the sense of calm and mindfulness.

Group Energy: Practicing yoga with a group of like-minded individuals can create a sense of community and support as you embark on your wellness journey.

Relaxation and Stress Reduction: Beach yoga is known for its stress-relief benefits, as it combines the physical postures of yoga with the tranquility of the beach environment.

Variety of Classes: Depending on the instructor and studio, you may have the option to choose from different styles of yoga, such as Vinyasa, Hatha, or even meditation-focused classes.

Accessibility: Beach yoga is accessible to practitioners of various skill levels, making it a welcoming activity for both beginners and experienced yogis.

Equipment: Some yoga classes provide yoga mats and props, but it's a good idea to bring your own if you have them.

Check Schedule: Be sure to check the schedule for local beach yoga classes and arrive a little early to secure your spot.

Morning beach yoga classes in the St. Petersburg area offer a unique and refreshing way to rejuvenate your body, mind, and spirit. Whether you're seeking relaxation, increased flexibility, or a sense of inner peace, the beach environment enhances the benefits of your yoga practice and provides a memorable and soothing experience.

53. Play frisbee at a beach park.

Playing frisbee at a beach park in the St. Petersburg area is a fun and active way to enjoy the sandy shores and ocean breeze. Here's what you can expect when you play frisbee at a beach park:

Sandy Beaches: The St. Petersburg area boasts several beautiful sandy beaches along the Gulf of Mexico, providing ample space for a game of frisbee.

Scenic Setting: The beach provides a stunning backdrop for your frisbee game, with the ocean waves, blue skies, and sandy shore creating a picturesque environment.

Family-Friendly: Frisbee is a family-friendly activity, making it suitable for all ages and a great way to bond with loved ones.

Casual Fun: Playing frisbee at the beach is generally a relaxed and casual activity, perfect for socializing and having a good time with friends and family.

Exercise: It's a great way to get some exercise while enjoying the outdoors, whether you're diving for catches or sprinting in the sand.

Team Play: You can play one-on-one or with teams, so it's adaptable to the number of participants.

Sun and Fun: The sunny and warm Florida weather makes playing frisbee at the beach a delightful outdoor activity year-round.

Social Gatherings: Beach frisbee is a popular pastime, and you may find other beachgoers willing to join in for a friendly game.

Beach Amenities: Many beaches offer amenities such as restrooms, picnic areas, and nearby eateries where you can grab refreshments.

Sun Protection: Don't forget to apply sunscreen, wear a hat, and stay hydrated to protect yourself from the sun's rays during your frisbee game.

Accessibility: Frisbee is an accessible activity for people of various skill levels, from beginners to experienced players.

Playing frisbee at a beach park in St. Petersburg offers a relaxing and enjoyable way to spend quality time with friends and family while taking in the coastal beauty and fresh air. Whether you're looking for a friendly match, a casual game, or a leisurely throw by the sea, the beach provides the perfect environment for frisbee fun.

54. Explore Maximo Park and its trails.

Exploring Maximo Park in St. Petersburg, Florida, and its scenic trails is a fantastic way to connect with nature, enjoy outdoor activities, and appreciate the beauty of the local environment. Here's what you can expect when you visit Maximo Park:

Natural Beauty: Maximo Park is known for its natural beauty, with lush greenery, waterways, and coastal habitats that provide a serene and picturesque setting.

Trails: The park features a network of trails that wind through the natural landscape, offering opportunities for hiking, walking, jogging, and birdwatching.

Scenic Views: As you traverse the trails, you'll encounter scenic views of the surrounding ecosystems, including wetlands, ponds, and possibly glimpses of local wildlife.

Birdwatching: Maximo Park is a great spot for birdwatching, with various bird species that call the park home or use it as a stopover during migration.

Wildlife Observation: The park is also home to other wildlife, including turtles, fish, and possibly small mammals.

Boardwalks: Some sections of the trails include boardwalks that take you through marshy areas, providing a unique perspective of the coastal ecosystem.

Educational Signage: Along the trails, you may find educational signage that offers information about the park's ecology, wildlife, and environmental conservation efforts.

Picnic Facilities: Maximo Park provides picnic tables and shelters where you can enjoy a meal with friends or family.

Fishing Opportunities: The park has fishing piers and areas where you can cast a line and try your luck at catching local fish.

Canoe and Kayak Launch: If you have your own canoe or kayak, there is a launch area in the park, allowing you to explore the waterways surrounding the park.

Restrooms: Restroom facilities are typically available for visitors' convenience.

Accessibility: The park is generally designed to be accessible to people of various abilities, ensuring that everyone can enjoy its amenities.

Maximo Park and its trails offer a peaceful and captivating environment for those who appreciate the outdoors, wildlife, and the natural beauty of the Florida Gulf Coast. Whether you're interested in hiking, birdwatching, or simply a tranquil walk in a natural setting, the trails of Maximo Park provide a welcoming and engaging experience in St. Petersburg.

55. Visit Crescent Lake Park.

Crescent Lake Park is a charming and serene urban park located in St. Petersburg, Florida. When you visit Crescent Lake Park, you can expect to enjoy a variety of activities and features in a tranquil setting. Here's what you can experience:

Crescent Lake: The park is centered around Crescent Lake, a picturesque and serene body of water that provides a beautiful backdrop for your visit.

Walking and Jogging Paths: Crescent Lake Park features paved walking and jogging paths that encircle the lake, making it an ideal location for a leisurely stroll, a brisk run, or a peaceful walk.

Fitness Stations: The park is equipped with fitness stations and exercise equipment along the paths, allowing visitors to engage in outdoor workouts while enjoying the scenery.

Playground: Crescent Lake Park includes a playground area, making it a family-friendly destination where children can have fun and play.

Picnic Areas: The park offers picnic tables and open spaces where you can enjoy a meal or snacks with family or friends.

Dog-Friendly: Leashed dogs are welcome in the park, providing an opportunity to enjoy the outdoors with your furry companions.

Wildlife Observation: The park's location near the lake provides opportunities for birdwatching and observing local wildlife, including ducks and other waterfowl.

Sunset Views: Crescent Lake Park is known for its stunning sunsets. It's a popular spot to watch the sun dip below the horizon.

Botanical Garden: The park is home to the St. Petersburg's Historical Society Botanical Gardens, where you can explore a variety of plants and garden settings.

Amphitheater: The park includes a small amphitheater that occasionally hosts events, concerts, and community gatherings.

Accessibility: Crescent Lake Park is designed to be accessible for people of various abilities, ensuring that everyone can enjoy its amenities.

Nearby Restaurants: The park is conveniently located near a variety of restaurants and cafes where you can grab a meal or a refreshing beverage.

Crescent Lake Park is a peaceful and inviting green space that provides a range of recreational opportunities and a calming atmosphere. Whether you're interested in a nature walk, a family picnic, exercise, or simply a place to unwind and enjoy the views, Crescent Lake Park offers a serene and welcoming experience in the heart of St. Petersburg.

56.Attend one of the city's frequent festivals.

St. Petersburg, Florida, is known for its vibrant and diverse festival scene, offering a wide array of cultural, artistic, and community events throughout the year. When you attend one of the city's frequent festivals, you can expect a lively and engaging experience. Here are some of the types of festivals you might encounter:

Arts and Culture Festivals: St. Petersburg hosts numerous arts and culture festivals celebrating various forms of creativity, including visual arts, music, dance, and theater. The SHINE Mural Festival, for example, showcases incredible street art throughout the city.

Food and Drink Festivals: The city is renowned for its culinary scene, and food festivals feature a wide range of delectable dishes, craft beers, and wines. The St. Pete Wine and Food Festival and the Ribfest are just a couple of examples.

Music Festivals: St. Petersburg offers an eclectic mix of music festivals, featuring local and international artists performing a variety of genres, from jazz and blues to rock and electronic music.

Community and Family Festivals: Numerous family-friendly festivals provide entertainment and activities for all ages, including parades, craft fairs, and holiday celebrations.

Film Festivals: Film enthusiasts can enjoy various film festivals, showcasing independent films, documentaries, and international cinema.

Environmental and Wellness Festivals: St. Petersburg also hosts events that promote environmental awareness, sustainability, and wellness, such as Earth Day celebrations and yoga festivals.

Pride Festivals: The city's LGBTQ+ community hosts Pride festivals, parades, and related events, celebrating diversity, inclusivity, and equality.

Holiday Festivals: St. Petersburg comes alive during holidays like Halloween, Christmas, and New Year's Eve with themed festivals, light displays, and fireworks.

Sports Festivals: The area hosts sports-related festivals and events, including regattas, triathlons, and soccer tournaments.

Artisan and Craft Festivals: Craft fairs and artisan markets are common, allowing you to discover unique handmade goods and local craftsmanship.

When you attend one of these festivals in St. Petersburg, you can immerse yourself in the local culture, connect with the community, and enjoy a range of entertainment, art, food, and activities. Be sure to check the local event calendar to find out about upcoming festivals and plan your visit accordingly.

57.Take part in the annual St. Pete Pride Parade.

Taking part in the annual St. Pete Pride Parade is a wonderful way to celebrate diversity, support LGBTQ+ rights, and enjoy a lively and inclusive community event. Here's what you can expect when you participate in the St. Pete Pride Parade:

Celebration of Diversity: The St. Pete Pride Parade is a celebration of the LGBTQ+ community and its diversity. It's a time to embrace and support people of all gender identities and sexual orientations.

Colorful Displays: The parade features vibrant and colorful displays, floats, costumes, and decorations that create a festive and joyful atmosphere.

Inclusivity: The event is open to everyone, regardless of their sexual orientation or gender identity. Allies and supporters are encouraged to join in and show their solidarity.

Community Unity: The parade fosters a sense of unity and togetherness within the community, as well as with allies and friends who come out to support LGBTQ+ rights.

Entertainment: You can expect various forms of entertainment, including music, dance, performances, and artistic expressions that reflect the LGBTQ+ culture.

Marching and Participation: Participants in the parade can include LGBTQ+ organizations, local businesses, community groups, schools, churches, and individuals who want to take part in the festivities.

Supporting LGBTQ+ Causes: The St. Pete Pride Parade serves as an important platform for raising awareness and funds for LGBTQ+ causes, including advocacy, support services, and initiatives.

Positive Energy: The parade exudes a positive and uplifting energy, fostering an environment where people can feel free to express themselves and be proud of who they are.

Educational Opportunities: The parade can offer opportunities for education and awareness about LGBTQ+ issues, rights, and challenges.

Community Engagement: It's a great chance to engage with the LGBTQ+ community, learn about its history, and support efforts for a more inclusive society.

Participating in the St. Pete Pride Parade is a memorable and impactful experience that allows you to stand in solidarity with the LGBTQ+ community and celebrate love, acceptance, and diversity. If you're interested in taking part, be sure to check the event's official website or contact the organizers for details on registration and participation in the parade.

58.Explore the Saturday Morning Market.

Exploring the Saturday Morning Market in St. Petersburg is a delightful way to experience the city's vibrant community, local flavors, and artisan products. Here's what you can expect when you visit the market:

Local Vendors: The Saturday Morning Market is a gathering of local vendors, farmers, artisans, and entrepreneurs who showcase their goods and products. You'll find a wide range of items, from fresh produce to handmade crafts.

Fresh Produce: The market features an abundance of fresh fruits and vegetables, allowing you to shop for locally grown, organic, and seasonal produce.

Artisanal Foods: You can savor a variety of artisanal and gourmet foods, including baked goods, pastries, cheeses, sauces, spices, and international cuisine.

Crafts and Art: Local artisans display their handmade crafts, artwork, jewelry, clothing, and unique creations, making it a perfect place to find one-of-a-kind souvenirs and gifts.

Live Music: Many markets include live musical performances, creating a lively and entertaining atmosphere as you shop and explore.

Food Trucks: Food trucks and vendors offer a diverse selection of ready-to-eat meals and snacks, from global cuisine to local specialties.

Community Atmosphere: The Saturday Morning Market provides an opportunity to engage with the community, connect with locals, and experience the warmth and friendliness of St. Petersburg.

Pet-Friendly: Some markets are pet-friendly, so you can bring your furry friends along for the outing.

Educational Experiences: The market occasionally hosts educational events, cooking demonstrations, gardening tips, and more, providing opportunities to learn and explore.

Seasonal Themes: Depending on the time of year, you might encounter special themes or holiday markets with festive decorations and seasonal treats.

Social Gathering: It's a popular gathering spot for locals and visitors alike, making it an excellent place to socialize, meet friends, and enjoy the weekend.

Supporting Local: By shopping at the Saturday Morning Market, you're supporting local businesses and contributing to the sustainability of the community.

Visiting the Saturday Morning Market is not only a chance to shop for fresh and unique products but also an opportunity to immerse yourself in the local culture, savor the flavors of St. Petersburg, and enjoy a lively and community-oriented atmosphere. Be sure to check the market's schedule, location, and any special events or themes before your visit.

59.Attend the Mainsail Arts Festival.

Attending the Mainsail Arts Festival in St. Petersburg is a fantastic way to immerse yourself in the world of art, culture, and creativity. Here's what you can expect when you visit the Mainsail Arts Festival:

Artistic Diversity: The Mainsail Arts Festival showcases a wide range of art forms and mediums, including paintings, sculptures, ceramics, jewelry, glasswork, photography, and more. The festival celebrates both traditional and contemporary art.

Juried Exhibition: The festival features a juried art exhibition, where artists submit their work for evaluation by a panel of judges. This ensures the highest quality of art on display.

Meet the Artists: It's an excellent opportunity to meet the artists in person, ask questions, and gain insights into their creative processes.

Art Sales: Many of the displayed artworks are available for purchase, allowing you to acquire unique pieces to enhance your art collection or decorate your home.

Entertainment: The festival often includes live entertainment, such as music performances, dance, and cultural presentations that add to the vibrant atmosphere.

Food and Beverage: Food vendors offer a variety of culinary delights, while beverage stations serve refreshments to keep you energized during your visit.

Interactive Art: Some art installations are interactive, providing a hands-on experience and opportunities for creativity.

Family-Friendly: The Mainsail Arts Festival is family-friendly, and children can engage in art-related activities and hands-on projects.

Educational Programs: The festival frequently hosts educational programs, workshops, and demonstrations for those interested in the creative process.

Cultural Enrichment: It's a chance to immerse yourself in the local art scene, appreciate the city's cultural diversity, and explore different artistic styles and techniques.

Scenic Location: The festival typically takes place in a scenic outdoor setting, such as a waterfront park, offering picturesque views and a pleasant environment for art appreciation.

Community Engagement: By attending the Mainsail Arts Festival, you become part of the local arts community, supporting artists and contributing to the cultural vibrancy of St. Petersburg.

Whether you're an art enthusiast, a collector, or simply someone who enjoys the beauty and creativity of fine art, the Mainsail Arts Festival offers a rich and inspiring experience. Be sure to check the festival's schedule and location, as well as any special events or exhibitions that may coincide with your visit.

60.Enjoy Localtopia, a celebration of local businesses.

Enjoying Localtopia in St. Petersburg is a wonderful way to support the community, discover local businesses, and immerse yourself in the city's unique culture. Here's what you can expect when you participate in Localtopia:

Local Business Showcase: Localtopia is a celebration of St. Petersburg's diverse and vibrant local businesses. You can explore a wide range of shops, boutiques, restaurants, breweries, and artisanal products.

Community Engagement: The event fosters community engagement by bringing residents and visitors together to celebrate local entrepreneurship and creativity.

Art and Craft Vendors: You'll find a variety of art and craft vendors displaying their creations, from handmade jewelry and clothing to unique artworks and home decor.

Food and Drink: Local restaurants, food trucks, and breweries often participate, offering a delicious array of culinary delights and locally brewed beverages.

Live Entertainment: Localtopia typically features live music, performances, and entertainment that contribute to the lively and festive atmosphere.

Family-Friendly: The event is family-friendly, with activities and attractions suitable for all ages, making it a great outing for families.

Interactive Experiences: Some businesses and vendors may offer interactive experiences, workshops, or demonstrations that allow you to get hands-on and learn more about their products or services.

Community Initiatives: Localtopia often serves as a platform for community initiatives, including sustainability efforts, neighborhood revitalization, and social causes.

Art and Culture: You can explore the local art scene, discover emerging artists, and appreciate the city's unique cultural offerings.

Supporting Local: By attending Localtopia and shopping from local businesses, you're directly supporting the community and contributing to the growth of St. Petersburg's economy.

Networking Opportunities: The event provides opportunities to connect with local business owners, artists, and like-minded individuals who share an appreciation for the city's culture and entrepreneurship.

Sustainability: Many local businesses at Localtopia emphasize sustainability, using eco-friendly practices and offering products that promote a greener lifestyle.

Attending Localtopia is a fun and meaningful way to explore St. Petersburg's entrepreneurial spirit, culture, and creativity. Whether you're looking for unique gifts, delicious cuisine, or simply want to engage with the local community, this celebration of local businesses is an event that offers a memorable and enriching experience. Be sure to check the event's schedule, location, and any special highlights before your visit.

61.Experience the SunLit Festival.

Experiencing the SunLit Festival in St. Petersburg is a literary and cultural adventure that celebrates the written word, authors, and the vibrant literary scene of the city. Here's what you can expect when you participate in the SunLit Festival:

Literary Events: The SunLit Festival features a wide range of literary events, including author readings, book signings, lectures, workshops, and panel discussions.

Bookish Gatherings: You'll have the opportunity to connect with fellow book lovers, writers, and avid readers, creating a sense of community among literary enthusiasts.

Local and Visiting Authors: The festival often hosts both local authors and well-known writers from various genres, providing opportunities to meet and engage with literary talents.

Travel to St. Petersburg Florida

Poetry Readings: Poetry readings and spoken word performances are an integral part of the festival, allowing you to savor the beauty of language and creative expression.

Book Releases: It's a platform for the release of new books and the promotion of literary works by local and national authors.

Workshops and Educational Programs: The festival may offer writing workshops, discussions on literary topics, and educational programs for aspiring writers and literature enthusiasts.

Visual Arts and Literature: Some events incorporate visual arts and interactive exhibits that bridge the gap between the written word and visual expression.

Book Swap and Sales: You might find book swaps, sales, and rare book collections that cater to book collectors and those seeking literary treasures.

Live Performances: The festival occasionally includes live performances that blend literature with music, theater, and multimedia experiences.

Children's and Young Adult Literature: Families and young readers can enjoy events and activities related to children's and young adult literature.

Bookstore and Publisher Presence: Local bookstores, publishers, and independent presses often participate in the festival, creating a marketplace for book browsing and shopping.

Cultural Diversity: The SunLit Festival showcases the diverse cultural and literary heritage of St. Petersburg and the Tampa Bay region.

Participating in the SunLit Festival is an enriching and inspiring experience for anyone who appreciates the written word, from avid readers and writers to those who simply enjoy the magic of storytelling. Be sure to check the festival's schedule, locations, and any special guests or themes that may enhance your literary journey.

62.Visit the St. Petersburg International Folk Fair.

Visiting the St. Petersburg International Folk Fair is a cultural experience that allows you to explore the rich tapestry of world cultures, traditions, and diversity. Here's what you can expect when you attend the Folk Fair:

Cultural Diversity: The Folk Fair is a celebration of cultural diversity, featuring displays, performances, and exhibits from various countries and regions.

International Pavilion: You can explore different international pavilions, each dedicated to a specific country or culture. These pavilions typically feature art, artifacts, traditional clothing, and information about the country's heritage.

Traditional Performances: Enjoy a variety of traditional performances, including music, dance, and theatrical presentations, showcasing the vibrant traditions of different cultures.

Cuisine: The Folk Fair often includes a culinary component, allowing you to savor international flavors with a wide range of delicious dishes, snacks, and beverages from around the world.

Arts and Crafts: You'll find artisanal products, handicrafts, and cultural souvenirs that reflect the artistic traditions of the participating countries.

Interactive Activities: Many pavilions offer interactive activities and workshops that allow you to learn about traditional customs, art, and craftsmanship.

Global Fashion: Explore traditional clothing, costumes, and fashion from various cultures, and perhaps even have the opportunity to try on and appreciate these beautiful garments.

Educational Exhibits: The Folk Fair often includes educational exhibits that provide insights into the history, geography, and culture of the participating countries.

Cultural Exchange: The event promotes cultural exchange and fosters understanding among diverse communities in St. Petersburg.

Family-Friendly: The Folk Fair is typically family-friendly, offering activities and experiences for all ages.

Live Music: Experience the joy of live music with performances that feature traditional instruments and melodies from around the world.

Community Unity: The Folk Fair emphasizes the unity and coexistence of different cultures, highlighting the importance of cultural diversity in the local community.

Visiting the St. Petersburg International Folk Fair is an opportunity to embark on a global journey without leaving the city, celebrating the beauty of cultural traditions and fostering a sense of unity among diverse communities. Be sure to check the fair's schedule, participating countries, and any special exhibits or performances that may enhance your cultural exploration.

63. Attend the St. Pete Seafood and Music Festival.

Attending the St. Pete Seafood and Music Festival is a delectable and entertaining experience that combines the flavors of the sea with live music and a festive atmosphere. Here's what you can expect when you participate in this festival:

Fresh Seafood: The festival showcases a mouthwatering array of fresh seafood, including shrimp, crab, oysters, fish, and various shellfish prepared in a variety of culinary styles.

Seafood Dishes: You can savor a diverse menu of seafood dishes, from seafood gumbo to lobster rolls, fish tacos, and shrimp scampi, created by local chefs and food vendors.

Music Performances: The festival features live music performances by local and regional artists, offering a backdrop of lively tunes that add to the festive atmosphere.

Diverse Musical Genres: The musical lineup may include a diverse range of genres, such as blues, jazz, rock, and reggae, catering to a variety of musical tastes.

Local Bands: Often, local bands and musicians take the stage, providing a platform for emerging talents and showcasing the local music scene.

Craft Vendors: Beyond the seafood and music, you'll find craft vendors selling handmade goods, artisan products, and unique souvenirs.

Beverages: Refreshing beverages, including craft beers, wines, and cocktails, complement the seafood dishes and live music.

Family-Friendly: The festival is typically family-friendly, offering activities for children, ensuring that the whole family can enjoy the day.

Seafood Education: Some festivals provide opportunities to learn about sustainable fishing practices and the importance of preserving marine ecosystems.

Cooking Demonstrations: You might find cooking demonstrations and workshops, where chefs share their culinary expertise and secrets for preparing delicious seafood dishes.

Scenic Setting: The festival often takes place in a scenic outdoor setting, such as a waterfront park, providing picturesque views and a pleasant environment.

Community Engagement: By attending the St. Pete Seafood and Music Festival, you become part of the local community's celebration of seafood, music, and culture.

Attending this festival is not only a feast for your taste buds but also a chance to enjoy live music, appreciate local craftsmanship, and immerse yourself in the lively and convivial atmosphere of St. Petersburg. Be sure to check the festival's schedule, location, and any special events or themed activities that may enhance your experience.

64.Explore the St. Petersburg Power & Sailboat Show.

Exploring the St. Petersburg Power & Sailboat Show is an exciting experience for boating enthusiasts and those interested in marine lifestyle. Here's what you can expect when you visit the show:

Travel to St. Petersburg Florida

Boat Exhibits: The show features a wide array of powerboats and sailboats on display, ranging from small recreational boats to larger vessels and luxury yachts.

New Models: You can explore the latest boat models, including cutting-edge designs, technology, and features, presented by boat manufacturers and dealers.

Pre-Owned Boats: Many exhibitors also offer pre-owned boats for sale, providing a variety of options for those looking for a second-hand vessel.

Accessories and Equipment: Beyond boats, the show includes exhibitors showcasing marine accessories, equipment, and gear for boating and sailing.

Nautical Lifestyle: The show often highlights the nautical lifestyle, offering products related to fishing, water sports, apparel, and marine-themed home decor.

Expert Advice: Visitors have the opportunity to connect with industry experts, boat dealers, and experienced sailors who can provide advice and insights into boating and sailing.

On-Water Demonstrations: Some boat shows may offer on-water demonstrations and sea trials, allowing attendees to test the boats on the water.

Educational Seminars: The event may host educational seminars and workshops on various topics related to boating, sailing, and marine safety.

Entertainment: Live entertainment, including music performances and marine-themed shows, adds to the festive atmosphere of the event.

Food and Beverage: You can enjoy food vendors and refreshment options, making it convenient to spend the day exploring the boats and exhibits.

Family-Friendly: The boat show is often family-friendly, with activities and entertainment suitable for all ages.

Boat Ownership Information: For those considering boat ownership, the show can provide valuable information about financing, insurance, maintenance, and marina services.

Attending the St. Petersburg Power & Sailboat Show is a fantastic opportunity to immerse yourself in the world of boating and sailing, whether you're a seasoned sailor or a novice with a growing interest in maritime adventures. Be sure to check the show's schedule, location, and any special events or seminars that may enhance your visit.

65.Participate in the Tampa Bay Blues Festival.

Participating in the Tampa Bay Blues Festival is a soulful and musical journey that celebrates the blues genre, featuring renowned artists and a passionate community of blues enthusiasts. Here's what you can expect when you attend the festival:

Live Blues Performances: The festival features an outstanding lineup of blues musicians and bands, offering live performances that cover a wide spectrum of blues styles, from Delta blues to Chicago blues and contemporary interpretations.

World-Class Artists: Renowned blues artists, both national and international, often grace the festival's stage, providing unforgettable musical experiences.

Scenic Setting: The festival usually takes place in a picturesque outdoor location, such as a waterfront park, offering beautiful views and a relaxed environment.

Food and Beverages: You can savor a variety of food vendors and beverage options, including local culinary delights and refreshing drinks to complement the music.

Craft Vendors: Explore artisan craft vendors, showcasing handmade goods, art, and souvenirs, offering opportunities for shopping and supporting local artists.

Blues Workshops: Some festivals offer educational workshops and masterclasses that delve into the history, culture, and musical techniques of the blues.

Jam Sessions: You might encounter impromptu jam sessions or after-hours performances at nearby venues, providing additional opportunities to enjoy live blues music.

Community of Blues Enthusiasts: The festival brings together a community of passionate blues enthusiasts and music lovers, creating a friendly and welcoming atmosphere.

Family-Friendly: Many festivals are family-friendly, offering activities and entertainment suitable for all ages.

Blues Culture: Immerse yourself in the culture of the blues, with events that emphasize the history and significance of this influential musical genre.

Supporting Local Music: By attending the Tampa Bay Blues Festival, you support the local and national blues music scene and contribute to the sustainability of this rich musical tradition.

Late-Night Shows: After the main festival hours, you can often find late-night shows at nearby venues, extending the musical experience into the evening.

Participating in the Tampa Bay Blues Festival is not just a music event; it's a celebration of the blues genre's heritage and a chance to connect with fellow music enthusiasts. Whether you're a seasoned blues aficionado or someone curious about the blues, this festival offers an exceptional opportunity to appreciate this timeless and influential genre. Be sure to check the festival's schedule, location, and any special artists or activities that may enhance your blues experience.

66.Go to the St. Pete Beach Corey Area Craft Festival.

Visiting the St. Pete Beach Corey Area Craft Festival is a delightful way to explore the world of arts and crafts while enjoying the beautiful coastal setting of St. Pete Beach. Here's what you can expect when you attend the craft festival:

Artisan Vendors: The festival features a diverse array of artisan vendors, showcasing their handmade creations, including jewelry, ceramics, woodwork, paintings, textiles, and much more.

Unique Crafts: You'll have the opportunity to discover unique and one-of-a-kind crafts that make for special souvenirs, gifts, or home decor items.

Craft Demonstrations: Some vendors may offer craft demonstrations, providing insights into their creative processes and allowing you to see how certain items are made.

Artistic Expression: The festival celebrates artistic expression and craftsmanship, allowing you to appreciate the skills and talents of local and visiting artists.

Live Music: Enjoy live music performances that create a lively and festive atmosphere as you browse the craft booths and interact with vendors.

Food and Beverages: Food vendors often offer a selection of delicious culinary treats and beverages to keep you energized while you explore the festival.

Community Engagement: The craft festival fosters community engagement and brings together local residents and visitors in a convivial and welcoming atmosphere.

Family-Friendly: The event is family-friendly, with activities and attractions suitable for all ages, making it a great outing for families.

Scenic Location: St. Pete Beach's Corey Avenue area is a picturesque setting for the festival, offering the opportunity to enjoy the coastal ambiance and the nearby beach.

Supporting Local Artists: By attending the Corey Area Craft Festival, you support local artisans and crafters, contributing to the sustainability of the local arts scene.

Nautical and Coastal Themes: You may find craft items with nautical and coastal themes that are particularly suited to the beachside location.

Interactive Experiences: Some vendors offer interactive experiences, workshops, or DIY craft activities, allowing you to get hands-on and tap into your own creativity.

Exploring the Corey Area Craft Festival is a fantastic way to immerse yourself in the world of arts and crafts, discover unique and handmade treasures, and appreciate the skills and talents of local and visiting artisans. Be sure to check the festival's schedule, location, and any special themes or activities that may enhance your craft festival experience.

67.Attend the Firestone Grand Prix.

Attending the Firestone Grand Prix in St. Petersburg is an adrenaline-packed experience for motorsports enthusiasts and those who appreciate high-speed racing. Here's what you can expect when you attend this thrilling event:

IndyCar Racing: The Firestone Grand Prix is part of the NTT IndyCar Series, featuring some of the world's best open-wheel racing drivers competing in fast and high-performance cars.

Race Circuit: The event takes place on a challenging street circuit in the heart of downtown St. Petersburg, offering a unique and urban racing atmosphere.

Various Races: In addition to the main NTT IndyCar Series race, you can also expect support races featuring different classes of racecars, including Indy Lights and sports cars, adding variety to the weekend's racing schedule.

Exciting On-Track Action: Witness high-speed wheel-to-wheel racing, daring overtakes, and intense competition as drivers navigate the tight street course.

Family-Friendly: The Firestone Grand Prix is family-friendly, with activities and entertainment suitable for all ages, making it a great outing for families.

Paddock Access: Some ticket options grant you access to the paddock, where you can get up close to the race teams, drivers, and their cars, providing an inside look at the world of motorsports.

Autograph Sessions: Meet and greet sessions with drivers and opportunities for autographs can be part of the event, allowing you to interact with the racing stars.

Food and Beverage Options: Enjoy a variety of food and beverage options, including local cuisine, as you watch the races and explore the event grounds.

Interactive Exhibits: Many racing-themed interactive exhibits and displays are available, allowing you to learn more about the technology, history, and culture of motorsports.

Vendor Booths: Explore vendor booths featuring racing memorabilia, merchandise, and motorsports-related products.

Entertainment: Beyond the racing, the event may include live entertainment, music, and activities to keep the excitement going.

Scenic Location: St. Petersburg's street circuit offers picturesque views of the city and the waterfront, providing a beautiful backdrop for the races.

Attending the Firestone Grand Prix is not just a motorsports event; it's a celebration of speed, precision, and the thrill of racing. Whether you're a seasoned motorsports fan or someone new to the world of racing, this event offers an exhilarating and unforgettable experience. Be sure to check the race schedule, ticket options, and any special activities or meet-and-greet opportunities that may enhance your Grand Prix experience.

68.Discover the St. Pete Wine & Food Festival.

Discovering the St. Pete Wine & Food Festival is a delightful journey into the world of culinary excellence, fine wines, and gastronomic experiences. Here's what you can expect when you attend this culinary festival:

Wine Tastings: The festival features an impressive selection of wines from various regions, allowing you to sample a wide array of varietals, including red, white, sparkling, and dessert wines.

Gourmet Cuisine: Savor delectable gourmet dishes prepared by local chefs and restaurants, showcasing their culinary talents and creativity.

Pairing Demonstrations: Learn about the art of food and wine pairing through demonstrations and workshops by experts in the field, enhancing your appreciation of both.

Celebrity Chefs: The festival may host renowned celebrity chefs who offer cooking demonstrations, tips, and insights into the culinary world.

Local Flavors: Discover the flavors of St. Petersburg and the surrounding region through dishes that incorporate locally sourced ingredients.

Artisanal Foods: Beyond wine and gourmet cuisine, explore artisanal foods, specialty products, and delicacies from local and international purveyors.

Craft Beer and Spirits: In addition to wine, you may find craft beer and spirits tastings, providing a well-rounded beverage experience.

Educational Workshops: Attend educational workshops and seminars on various topics related to wine, food, and culinary culture, offering valuable insights for enthusiasts.

Live Entertainment: Enjoy live entertainment, including music, performances, and cultural presentations, that adds to the festival's lively atmosphere.

Interactive Experiences: Some festivals offer interactive experiences, such as cooking classes, wine blending sessions, and hands-on culinary activities.

Food Competitions: Witness or participate in culinary competitions and challenges that showcase the talents of local chefs and home cooks.

Food and Beverage Pairing Dinners: The festival often includes special dining experiences, such as food and wine pairing dinners, where you can enjoy multi-course meals with expertly matched wines.

Scenic Locations: Many wine and food festivals take place in picturesque settings, providing a beautiful backdrop for your culinary exploration.

Attending the St. Pete Wine & Food Festival is a culinary adventure that allows you to indulge in the finest flavors, learn from experts, and immerse yourself in the local and international food and wine culture. Whether you're a seasoned epicurean or someone with a burgeoning interest in the culinary world, this festival offers a memorable and flavorful experience. Be sure to check the festival's schedule, location, and any special dining events or celebrity chef appearances that may enhance your culinary journey.

69. Visit the annual Ribfest food and music festival.

Visiting the annual Ribfest food and music festival is a mouthwatering and musically rich experience that combines delicious barbecue with live music performances. Here's what you can expect when you attend Ribfest:

BBQ Ribs: Ribfest is all about mouthwatering barbecue ribs. Enjoy a variety of rib styles, sauces, and flavors prepared by both local and visiting pitmasters.

BBQ Competitions: Witness BBQ competitions where talented grillmasters showcase their skills and vie for awards in categories like best ribs, best sauce, and more.

Variety of Food: While ribs take the spotlight, you'll also find a range of other food vendors serving up a diverse selection of culinary delights, from smoked meats to sides and desserts.

Live Music: Ribfest typically features live music performances by a mix of local, national, and international artists across various musical genres, creating a lively and festive atmosphere.

Musical Headliners: Look forward to headlining acts and well-known bands or artists who take the stage, providing top-notch entertainment.

Arts and Crafts: Explore artisan and craft vendors offering unique and handmade products, from artwork to jewelry and more.

Family-Friendly: The event is often family-friendly, with activities and attractions suitable for all ages, making it a great outing for families.

Beer and Beverages: Enjoy a selection of craft beers, refreshments, and beverages to complement your BBQ feast and enhance the festival experience.

Entertainment: Beyond music, you may find entertainment options like carnival rides, games, and interactive exhibits.

Community Engagement: By attending Ribfest, you become part of the local community's celebration of BBQ culture and music, supporting both local businesses and charities, as many Ribfest events are charity fundraisers.

Rib Eating Contests: Some festivals include rib-eating contests where participants compete to see who can devour the most ribs in a given time.

Scenic Setting: The festival often takes place in a scenic outdoor location, providing a beautiful backdrop for the event and opportunities for relaxation and enjoyment.

Attending Ribfest is a flavorful and festive experience that brings together the love of BBQ, music, and community. Whether you're a BBQ connoisseur, a music lover, or someone who enjoys a good time, this festival offers an unforgettable and delicious journey. Be sure to check the festival's schedule, location, and any special musical headliners or BBQ competitions that may enhance your Ribfest experience.

70.Enjoy the SHINE Mural Festival.

The SHINE Mural Festival in St. Petersburg is a vibrant celebration of street art and muralism, turning the city's public spaces into an open-air art gallery. Here's what you can expect when you enjoy the SHINE Mural Festival:

Mural Creation: Witness talented local and international artists transform building walls and public spaces into stunning works of art through the creation of large-scale murals.

Street Art Styles: Experience a diverse range of street art styles, from realistic and figurative pieces to abstract and contemporary art, each offering a unique perspective and visual impact.

Interactive Art: Some murals and installations may be interactive, allowing you to engage with the artwork, take photos, or even become part of the art experience.

Walking Tours: Guided walking tours and mural tours are often available, providing insights into the artists' techniques, inspirations, and the stories behind each mural.

Community Involvement: SHINE often involves the local community in the mural-making process, fostering a sense of shared ownership and pride in the artwork.

Art Workshops: The festival may offer art workshops, allowing you to try your hand at various street art techniques and create your own small-scale artwork.

Live Art Demonstrations: Some artists may perform live art demonstrations, giving you the opportunity to watch their creative process in action.

Artistic Expression: SHINE showcases a wide variety of artistic expression, from social and political statements to themes of culture, nature, and urban life.

Local and International Artists: The festival often hosts both local and international artists, contributing to the global street art community's diversity.

Street Art Culture: Dive into the culture of street art, learning about its history, significance, and impact on urban landscapes.

Photography Opportunities: The murals provide fantastic photo opportunities, making it a great place for photography enthusiasts to capture striking images.

Festival Atmosphere: SHINE creates a lively and festive atmosphere in the city, bringing people together to celebrate art, culture, and creativity.

Enjoying the SHINE Mural Festival is a wonderful way to explore the intersection of art and the urban environment, appreciate the talents of street artists, and immerse yourself in the vibrant and dynamic world of public art. Be sure to check the festival's schedule, mural locations, and any special events or workshops that may enhance your experience.

71. Visit the Saturday Artwalk in the Warehouse Arts District.

Visiting the Saturday Artwalk in the Warehouse Arts District is an opportunity to immerse yourself in the local art scene, explore galleries and studios, and connect with artists. Here's what you can expect when you attend the Saturday Artwalk:

Art Galleries: Discover a diverse range of art galleries and studios showcasing various forms of art, including paintings, sculptures, photography, and more.

Local Artists: Interact with local artists, as many of them are present during the Artwalk to discuss their work, share insights, and answer questions.

Art Exhibitions: Enjoy rotating art exhibitions that feature both established and emerging artists, providing fresh and inspiring perspectives with each visit.

Art for Sale: Many of the artworks displayed are available for purchase, making the Artwalk a great opportunity to acquire original art for your collection.

Live Demonstrations: Some artists may offer live demonstrations of their artistic techniques, allowing you to witness the creative process in action.

Open Studios: Explore open studios where artists create their work, providing a behind-the-scenes look at the art-making process.

Artwork Variety: The Saturday Artwalk typically features a variety of artistic styles and mediums, catering to a wide range of artistic preferences.

Meet the Community: The Artwalk is not only an opportunity to engage with artists but also a chance to connect with fellow art enthusiasts and the local creative community.

Art Events: The Warehouse Arts District may host special art-related events, such as art talks, workshops, and themed exhibitions during the Artwalk.

Food and Beverage: Some Artwalks include food and beverage vendors, allowing you to enjoy refreshments while exploring the art venues.

Local Culture: Immerse yourself in the local culture and gain a deeper appreciation for the art scene in St. Petersburg.

Scenic Locations: The Warehouse Arts District often has scenic and artistic environments that provide a visually appealing backdrop for the Artwalk.

The Saturday Artwalk is a fantastic way to support local artists, discover new talent, and enrich your artistic sensibilities. Whether you're a seasoned art collector or someone with a burgeoning interest in the arts, this event offers a vibrant and creative experience. Be sure to check the Artwalk's schedule, participating galleries, and any special exhibitions or events that may enhance your visit.

72. Experience the SHINE Mural Festival.

Experiencing the SHINE Mural Festival in St. Petersburg is a dynamic and artistic journey through the city's streets, filled with colorful and expressive murals. Here's what you can look forward to when you participate in the SHINE Mural Festival:

Street Art Transformation: Watch as the cityscape transforms with large-scale murals created by talented local and international artists. Each mural brings new life to public spaces.

Diverse Art Styles: SHINE features an array of street art styles, from realistic and figurative pieces to abstract and contemporary art, showcasing a wide range of artistic expression.

Walking Tours: Guided walking tours and mural tours are often available, providing insights into the artists' creative processes, inspirations, and the stories behind the murals.

Community Engagement: Many of the murals are created with community involvement, fostering a sense of shared ownership and pride in the artwork among local residents.

Interactive Art: Some murals are interactive, allowing you to engage with the artwork, take photos, and even become part of the art experience.

Artistic Expression: SHINE murals often explore themes of culture, nature, social issues, and urban life, providing meaningful and thought-provoking pieces of public art.

Local and International Artists: The festival brings together a diverse group of artists, both local and international, contributing to the global street art community's richness.

Scenic Locations: SHINE murals can be found in various scenic locations throughout the city, enhancing the visual appeal of St. Petersburg.

Family-Friendly: The festival is family-friendly, with activities and attractions suitable for all ages, making it an ideal outing for families.

Photography Opportunities: The vibrant and striking murals offer fantastic opportunities for photography, making it a favorite destination for photographers.

Street Art Culture: Dive into the culture of street art, learning about its history, significance, and the impact of street art on urban landscapes.

Festival Atmosphere: SHINE creates a lively and festive atmosphere in the city, drawing people together to celebrate art, culture, and creativity.

Experiencing the SHINE Mural Festival is an exciting way to explore the intersection of art and the urban environment, appreciate the talents of street artists, and immerse yourself in the vibrant and dynamic world of public art. Whether you're an art enthusiast, a street art aficionado, or someone with a growing interest in urban art, this festival offers an unforgettable and visually captivating experience. Be sure to check the festival's schedule, mural locations, and any special events or workshops that may enhance your SHINE Mural Festival experience.

73.Explore the Gandy Bridge Trail.

Exploring the Gandy Bridge Trail is a scenic outdoor adventure that offers beautiful views and recreational opportunities in the St. Petersburg area. Here's what you can expect when you visit the Gandy Bridge Trail:

Bridge Crossing: The trail includes a portion of the Gandy Bridge, which spans Tampa Bay, providing a unique and scenic setting for your outdoor excursion.

Biking and Walking: The trail is popular among both cyclists and pedestrians, offering a dedicated path for biking and walking, allowing you to enjoy the outdoors at your own pace.

Scenic Views: As you cross the bridge, you'll be treated to breathtaking views of Tampa Bay, the surrounding waters, and the skyline of St. Petersburg and Tampa.

Sunset Views: The Gandy Bridge Trail is particularly famous for its stunning sunset views, making it a favorite spot for evening walks and rides.

Fishing: Many people come to the bridge for fishing. You can cast your line into the bay from designated fishing spots along the trail.

Picnic Areas: Some sections of the trail have designated picnic areas where you can take a break and enjoy a meal or a snack while taking in the views.

Wildlife Viewing: Keep an eye out for local wildlife, including birds, dolphins, and marine life, which are often visible in the bay.

Fitness and Recreation: The trail is not only a scenic route but also a great place for fitness enthusiasts to get some exercise while enjoying the outdoors.

Access to Local Parks: The Gandy Bridge Trail connects to several local parks, allowing you to extend your outdoor adventure by exploring nearby green spaces.

Dog-Friendly: The trail is often dog-friendly, making it a popular spot for dog walkers and a great place to enjoy the outdoors with your furry friend.

Safety: The trail is well-maintained and often features safety features, such as barriers and lighting, making it a comfortable and secure outdoor experience.

Connecting Communities: The Gandy Bridge Trail connects the communities of St. Petersburg and Tampa, providing a convenient and picturesque route for commuters and outdoor enthusiasts.

Exploring the Gandy Bridge Trail is a wonderful way to experience the beauty of Tampa Bay, stay active, and connect with nature while taking in breathtaking views. Whether you're a cyclist, walker, nature enthusiast, or someone looking for a tranquil place to enjoy the sunset, this trail offers a scenic and relaxing experience. Be sure to check the trail's access points, parking, and any specific rules or regulations before your visit.

74.Bike the Pinellas Trail.

Biking the Pinellas Trail is a fantastic way to explore the natural beauty and urban landscapes of Pinellas County. Here's what you can expect when you embark on a biking adventure along the Pinellas Trail:

Scenic Route: The Pinellas Trail covers approximately 38 miles, winding through diverse landscapes, including urban areas, lush parks, coastal scenery, and serene neighborhoods.

Biking and Walking: The trail is designed for both cyclists and pedestrians, providing a dedicated and safe path for biking while accommodating walkers and joggers as well.

Travel to St. Petersburg Florida

Diverse Terrain: As you pedal along the trail, you'll encounter a variety of terrains, from flat and straight stretches to gentle hills, making it suitable for bikers of different skill levels.

Stunning Natural Beauty: The Pinellas Trail takes you through picturesque landscapes, including shaded canopies of trees, wetlands, scenic bridges, and waterfront views.

Cultural Stops: Along the route, you'll find opportunities to explore local culture, including historical sites, public art, and charming communities.

Rest Stops: The trail features several rest areas with benches, water fountains, and restroom facilities, offering a convenient break during your ride.

Wildlife Sightings: Keep an eye out for local wildlife, such as birds, turtles, and even the occasional alligator in the wetland areas.

Fitness and Recreation: The Pinellas Trail is an ideal destination for fitness enthusiasts, offering a chance to enjoy nature while getting a great workout.

Family-Friendly: The trail is family-friendly, with a safe and accessible path for riders of all ages. It's a wonderful option for a family biking adventure.

Connecting Communities: The trail links several communities within Pinellas County, making it a convenient and enjoyable way to explore the area and connect with local culture.

Dog-Friendly: Many sections of the trail are dog-friendly, so you can bring your canine companion along for the ride.

Events and Festivals: Keep an eye out for special events and festivals that may take place along the trail, providing additional opportunities for fun and community engagement.

Biking the Pinellas Trail is a delightful and active way to experience the beauty and culture of Pinellas County. Whether you're a seasoned cyclist or someone looking for a leisurely ride through scenic landscapes, this trail offers an enriching and immersive experience. Be sure to check the trail's access points, parking options, and any specific rules or guidelines before you begin your biking journey.

75. Walk or run along the Legacy Trail.

Walking or running along the Legacy Trail is a refreshing and active way to explore the natural beauty of Sarasota County. Here's what you can expect when you walk or run along this picturesque trail:

Scenic Path: The Legacy Trail is a 12.5-mile long, paved trail that winds through a diverse range of environments, including woodlands, wetlands, and suburban areas.

Walking and Running: The trail is designed for both walkers and runners, offering a dedicated path that provides a safe and comfortable environment for exercise.

Varied Terrain: You'll encounter a mix of terrain, with some parts of the trail being flat and straight while others feature gentle slopes, making it suitable for individuals of different fitness levels.

Natural Beauty: The Legacy Trail takes you through lush and scenic landscapes, featuring native vegetation, wildlife sightings, and lovely waterway views.

Rest Stops: Along the trail, you'll find rest areas equipped with benches, picnic tables, and water fountains, offering convenient spots to take a break and enjoy the surroundings.

Birdwatching: Keep an eye out for the various bird species that call this area home, making it a popular spot for birdwatching.

Fitness and Recreation: The trail provides an excellent opportunity for outdoor exercise, whether you prefer brisk walking, jogging, or running.

Dog-Friendly: Many sections of the Legacy Trail are dog-friendly, allowing you to bring your four-legged companion along for a run or walk.

Community Connections: The trail connects several communities in Sarasota County, making it a convenient way to explore the area and discover local culture.

Family-Friendly: The Legacy Trail is family-friendly, offering a safe and enjoyable environment for children and adults alike.

Health and Well-Being: Taking a walk or run along the trail is not only a form of exercise but also a way to de-stress, rejuvenate, and enhance your overall well-being.

Events and Gatherings: Keep an eye out for special events, group runs, and community gatherings that may take place along the trail, providing opportunities to meet like-minded individuals and share in the experience.

Walking or running along the Legacy Trail is an invigorating and peaceful way to connect with nature, embrace a healthy lifestyle, and engage with the local community. Whether you're a dedicated runner or someone looking for a serene walk, this trail offers an enriching and immersive experience. Be sure to check the trail's access points, parking options, and any specific rules or guidelines before you embark on your walking or running journey.

76.Hike at Boca Ciega Millennium Park.

Hiking at Boca Ciega Millennium Park is a great way to explore the natural beauty and biodiversity of this unique coastal park in Pinellas County. Here's what you can expect when you hike in Boca Ciega Millennium Park:

Trails for All Skill Levels: The park offers a variety of trails suitable for hikers of all skill levels, from easy strolls to more challenging paths for experienced hikers.

Scenic Beauty: Enjoy picturesque views of Boca Ciega Bay, lush mangrove forests, and diverse natural habitats as you hike through the park.

Wildlife Observation: Keep an eye out for a wide range of wildlife, including birds, fish, and possibly even dolphins and manatees in the bay.

Educational Opportunities: Interpretive signs and exhibits along the trails provide insights into the local flora and fauna, enhancing your hiking experience.

Picnic Areas: The park features designated picnic areas where you can take a break, enjoy a meal, and savor the coastal ambiance.

Observation Tower: Climb the observation tower for panoramic views of the surrounding environment, including the bay and nearby ecosystems.

Mangrove Boardwalk: Explore the mangrove boardwalk that meanders through a stunning mangrove forest, providing an up-close encounter with this unique coastal habitat.

Beach Access: Some trails lead to the park's sandy beach area, allowing you to relax by the bay or even dip your toes in the water.

Dog-Friendly: Boca Ciega Millennium Park is often dog-friendly, so you can bring your canine companion along for a hike.

Community Events: The park occasionally hosts community events, nature walks, and educational programs, providing opportunities to engage with the local community and learn more about the park's ecology.

Photography Opportunities: The park's diverse landscapes and scenic beauty offer excellent opportunities for nature and wildlife photography.

Relaxation and Tranquility: Whether you're looking for an active hike or a peaceful nature walk, Boca Ciega Millennium Park provides a serene and tranquil environment to connect with nature.

Hiking in Boca Ciega Millennium Park allows you to immerse yourself in the coastal beauty of Florida's Gulf Coast while enjoying a range of outdoor activities and the opportunity to observe diverse ecosystems. Be sure to check the park's hours of operation, trail maps, and any specific rules or guidelines before your visit.

77. Visit the Florida Orange Groves Winery.

Visiting the Florida Orange Groves Winery is a delightful experience that allows you to sample a unique range of tropical fruit wines and learn about the winemaking process in a beautiful setting. Here's what you can expect when you visit this winery:

Tropical Fruit Wines: The winery is known for producing a wide variety of fruit wines, many of which are made from tropical fruits like oranges, mangos, and guavas. You can taste these unique and flavorful creations.

Travel to St. Petersburg Florida

Wine Tasting: Enjoy a wine tasting experience where you can sample a selection of wines from their extensive menu. The tastings often include both dry and sweet wines, catering to a range of tastes.

Guided Tours: Some wineries offer guided tours of their facilities, giving you insights into the winemaking process, the history of the winery, and the fruit sources used in production.

Wine Shop: Explore the winery's on-site shop, where you can purchase your favorite wines, wine-related merchandise, and gourmet food products.

Scenic Setting: Many wineries are located in picturesque locations, providing a charming backdrop for your visit. The Florida Orange Groves Winery may offer a lovely outdoor area where you can relax and enjoy your wine.

Educational Experience: Learn about the art and science of winemaking, including the unique challenges and techniques involved in making fruit wines.

Pairings and Food: Some wineries offer food and wine pairings, allowing you to sample wines alongside delicious dishes or snacks that complement the flavors.

Local Culture: Immerse yourself in the local culture and history of Florida's citrus and fruit industry while exploring the winery.

Events and Festivals: Keep an eye out for special events and festivals that may be hosted by the winery, featuring live music, food vendors, and more.

Winery Tours: Some wineries provide guided tours of their vineyards or orchards, offering a closer look at the fruit-growing process.

Wine Education: Whether you're a wine enthusiast or a novice, you can often gain valuable insights into wine appreciation, from tasting techniques to food pairings.

Visiting the Florida Orange Groves Winery is an enjoyable way to experience the flavors of Florida's tropical fruits in a different form. Whether you're a wine connoisseur or someone looking to expand their palate, this winery offers a unique and tasty experience. Be sure to check the winery's operating hours, tour availability, and any special events or tastings that may enhance your visit.

78.Enjoy a brewery tour at local craft breweries.

Enjoying a brewery tour at local craft breweries in St. Petersburg, Florida is a fantastic way to explore the region's vibrant craft beer scene and gain insights into the brewing process. Here's what you can expect when you embark on brewery tours:

Craft Beer Tastings: Most brewery tours include tastings of a variety of craft beers produced on-site. You'll get to sample a range of beer styles, from IPAs to stouts, and potentially some experimental brews.

Behind-the-Scenes Look: Brewery tours typically take you behind the scenes to see the brewing equipment and learn about the brewing process, from mashing and fermenting to bottling or canning.

Knowledgeable Guides: Knowledgeable guides or brewers often lead the tours, sharing their expertise on the beer-making process, ingredients, and the history of the brewery.

Tasting Room Experience: Enjoy the ambiance of the brewery's tasting room, where you can relax, socialize, and savor your favorite brews.

Food Pairings: Some breweries offer food pairings with their beer, enhancing the tasting experience with delicious bites that complement the flavors of the brews.

Souvenir Merchandise: You may have the opportunity to purchase brewery merchandise, such as T-shirts, glassware, or even growlers to take your favorite beer home.

Local Culture: Dive into the local beer culture and connect with the community of craft beer enthusiasts.

Events and Festivals: Keep an eye out for special events and festivals hosted by the breweries, offering live music, food trucks, and themed celebrations.

Artistic Decor: Many craft breweries take pride in their artistic and creative décor, providing a unique and engaging atmosphere.

Community Engagement: Brewery tours often provide a platform for connecting with the local community and supporting small, independent businesses.

Pet-Friendly: Some breweries are pet-friendly, so you can bring your furry friend along for the tour.

Safety: Enjoy your tasting experience responsibly, and if you're planning on visiting multiple breweries, consider arranging for transportation to ensure safety.

Exploring local craft breweries in St. Petersburg offers a delightful journey through the world of artisanal beer, from the brewing process to the diverse range of flavors and styles available. Whether you're a beer enthusiast or someone looking to discover new tastes, brewery tours provide an enjoyable and educational experience. Be sure to check the breweries' tour schedules, any specific tasting packages, and any special events that may enhance your brewery tour adventure.

79. Take a coffee shop tour in downtown St. Petersburg.

Taking a coffee shop tour in downtown St. Petersburg is a delightful way to explore the city's coffee culture, sample different brews, and experience the unique ambiance of various coffee shops. Here's what you can expect on your coffee shop tour:

Diverse Coffee Selection: Each coffee shop has its own selection of coffee beans, roasting methods, and brewing techniques, allowing you to sample a wide range of flavors and coffee styles.

Café Ambiance: Explore the different atmospheres of each coffee shop, from cozy and intimate spaces to bustling and lively environments, offering diverse settings for your coffee enjoyment.

Local Art and Decor: Many coffee shops feature local art displays and unique decor, providing an artistic and creative backdrop for your coffee experience.

Barista Expertise: Interact with skilled baristas who are passionate about coffee and can provide recommendations based on your preferences.

Pastries and Snacks: Coffee shops often offer a variety of pastries, snacks, and light bites to complement your coffee selection.

Specialty Brews: Look for specialty brews, such as pour-overs, cold brews, and single-origin coffees, for a distinctive coffee-tasting experience.

Coffee Classes: Some coffee shops host classes or events where you can learn about the coffee-making process, from bean to cup.

Local and Sustainable Sourcing: Many coffee shops prioritize locally sourced and ethically traded coffee beans, promoting sustainability in the coffee industry.

Coffee Shop Hopping: Plan a route that takes you to several coffee shops in the area, allowing you to sample a variety of brews and discover hidden gems.

Live Music and Events: Some coffee shops host live music performances, open mic nights, and other events, creating a lively and entertaining atmosphere.

Community Engagement: Coffee shops are often hubs of local community activity, offering a space for people to meet, socialize, and work.

Outdoor Seating: Take advantage of outdoor seating areas if available, providing an opportunity to enjoy your coffee al fresco.

Exploring the coffee shops in downtown St. Petersburg offers a rich and flavorful journey through the city's coffee scene. Whether you're a coffee connoisseur or someone looking to savor the local coffee culture, a coffee shop tour provides an enjoyable and aromatic experience. Be sure to check the coffee shops' operating hours, any special brews or events, and their individual personalities to plan your coffee tour adventure.

80.Explore the Dade Battlefield Historic State Park.

Exploring the Dade Battlefield Historic State Park is a fascinating way to connect with Florida's history and natural beauty. Here's what you can expect when you visit this historic state park:

Travel to St. Petersburg Florida

Historical Significance: The park is named after the site of the Dade Massacre, a significant event in the Second Seminole War that occurred in 1835. Learn about this pivotal moment in Florida's history through interpretive exhibits and guided tours.

Visitor Center: Start your visit at the park's visitor center, where you can gather information, view exhibits, and speak with park rangers who can provide insights into the historical context of the site.

Educational Programs: The park often offers educational programs and events that delve into the history of the Dade Massacre, the Second Seminole War, and the area's indigenous culture.

Picnicking: Enjoy a picnic in the park's designated picnic areas. It's a great way to relax and refuel during your visit.

Hiking Trails: Explore the park's natural beauty by hiking on well-marked trails. The trails take you through pine flatwoods, sandhill, and scrub habitats, allowing you to appreciate Florida's diverse ecosystem.

Wildlife Viewing: Keep an eye out for native wildlife, including birds, deer, and various reptiles, as you hike and explore the park.

Battlefield Reenactments: Some events and festivals may feature historical reenactments of the Dade Massacre, bringing the past to life and offering a unique and immersive experience.

Camping: If you're looking for an extended outdoor experience, the park offers a campground with facilities for both tents and RVs.

Scenic Landscapes: Take in the beauty of the park's landscapes, which include open fields, forests, and serene nature areas, perfect for nature enthusiasts and photographers.

Stargazing: Dade Battlefield Historic State Park can be an excellent spot for stargazing, particularly if you visit during the evening.

Community Events: The park occasionally hosts community events, festivals, and cultural programs that provide additional opportunities for engagement and learning.

Family-Friendly: The park is family-friendly, making it a suitable destination for visitors of all ages.

Exploring the Dade Battlefield Historic State Park offers a chance to connect with history, nature, and the cultural heritage of Florida. Whether you're interested in history, outdoor recreation, or simply enjoying the scenic landscapes, this park provides a unique and enriching experience. Be sure to check the park's hours of operation, any special events, and any fees associated with your visit.

81.Discover the Lake Maggiore Environmental Education Center.

Discovering the Lake Maggiore Environmental Education Center is an educational and immersive experience that allows you to connect with nature and learn about the unique ecosystem of Lake Maggiore in St. Petersburg, Florida. Here's what you can expect when you visit this environmental education center:

Nature Trails: Explore the scenic nature trails that wind through the Lake Maggiore Park, offering opportunities for birdwatching, wildlife observation, and leisurely walks in a natural setting.

Educational Exhibits: The education center often features interactive exhibits and displays that provide insights into the local environment, wildlife, and conservation efforts.

Educational Programs: The center offers educational programs and workshops, catering to visitors of all ages. Learn about the ecology of Lake Maggiore, local flora and fauna, and conservation efforts.

Guided Tours: Guided tours are sometimes available, led by knowledgeable naturalists who can offer in-depth information about the park's ecology, history, and conservation initiatives.

Wildlife Viewing: Lake Maggiore Park is home to various wildlife species, including birds, turtles, and aquatic creatures. Bring your binoculars to enhance your wildlife viewing experience.

Botanical Gardens: Some environmental education centers include botanical gardens that showcase native and exotic plant species, allowing you to appreciate the diversity of the natural world.

Community Engagement: The center often hosts events and activities that engage the local community and promote environmental awareness and stewardship.

Family-Friendly: The Lake Maggiore Environmental Education Center is family-friendly, offering a range of programs and activities suitable for visitors of all ages.

Scenic Beauty: The park surrounding Lake Maggiore is visually stunning, providing an ideal backdrop for nature enthusiasts and photographers.

Conservation Initiatives: Learn about the ongoing conservation efforts and initiatives aimed at protecting Lake Maggiore's ecosystem and preserving its natural beauty.

Outdoor Recreation: In addition to educational activities, the park often offers opportunities for outdoor recreation, such as picnicking and fishing.

Volunteer Opportunities: Some centers provide information about volunteer opportunities, allowing you to get involved in conservation and environmental projects.

Visiting the Lake Maggiore Environmental Education Center offers an engaging way to appreciate the natural world, learn about local ecology, and support conservation efforts. Whether you're an environmental enthusiast, a nature lover, or someone interested in the educational and recreational aspects of the outdoors, this center provides a valuable and enriching experience. Be sure to check the center's hours of operation, any special programs, and any fees associated with your visit.

82. Visit the St. Petersburg Shuffleboard Club.

Visiting the St. Petersburg Shuffleboard Club is a unique and nostalgic experience that allows you to immerse yourself in the rich history of shuffleboard in St. Petersburg, Florida. Here's what you can expect when you visit this historic club:

Historical Significance: The St. Petersburg Shuffleboard Club is recognized as the world's largest and oldest shuffleboard club. It has a storied history that dates back to 1924.

Shuffleboard Courts: The club features a substantial number of shuffleboard courts, where you can watch or participate in shuffleboard games. The courts are maintained in excellent condition, offering a traditional shuffleboard experience.

Community and Social Engagement: The club has a strong sense of community and hosts a variety of social events, tournaments, and gatherings. It's an opportunity to connect with local residents and shuffleboard enthusiasts.

Educational Exhibits: The club often displays educational exhibits and information about the history of shuffleboard, the evolution of the sport, and its significance in St. Petersburg.

Tournaments: The club may host shuffleboard tournaments, giving you the chance to watch or even participate in competitive shuffleboard matches.

Lessons and Demonstrations: Some clubs offer lessons and demonstrations, particularly for newcomers or those looking to enhance their shuffleboard skills.

Art and Decor: The club's facilities often feature artistic decor and murals, creating a charming and retro atmosphere that transports you to a bygone era.

Picnic and Relaxation Areas: Enjoy the shaded picnic and relaxation areas surrounding the shuffleboard courts, making it an ideal spot for a leisurely afternoon.

Membership Opportunities: Some shuffleboard clubs offer memberships, which can provide access to additional benefits and social events.

Historical Tours: The club may offer historical tours that provide insights into the evolution of shuffleboard and the club's significance in the community.

Community Events: Keep an eye out for special events, festivals, and gatherings hosted by the club, which offer an opportunity to engage with local residents and visitors.

Family-Friendly: The St. Petersburg Shuffleboard Club is a family-friendly destination, suitable for all ages.

Visiting the St. Petersburg Shuffleboard Club is not just a leisurely pastime but also a journey back in time to explore the history and culture of shuffleboard in Florida. Whether you're a shuffleboard enthusiast, a history buff, or someone looking for a nostalgic and unique experience, this club provides an enriching and enjoyable outing. Be sure to check the club's hours of operation, any special events, and any fees associated with your visit.

83.Attend the St. Pete Beach Classic.

Attending the St. Pete Beach Classic is a fantastic way to participate in a lively and community-centered event in St. Pete Beach, Florida. Here's what you can expect when you attend this classic event:

Running Races: The St. Pete Beach Classic primarily features running races, including a variety of distances to cater to runners of different skill levels. From fun runs to half marathons, there's a race for everyone.

Scenic Courses: Enjoy running or walking along scenic routes that often include views of the beach, beautiful waterfront, and charming coastal neighborhoods.

Community Engagement: The event typically draws participants and spectators from the local community and beyond, providing a great opportunity to connect with other fitness enthusiasts and locals.

Fitness and Fun: Whether you're a seasoned runner or a novice, the St. Pete Beach Classic offers a fun and festive atmosphere that encourages physical activity and a healthy lifestyle.

Family-Friendly: Many races are family-friendly, so you can involve your entire family in the event. Some races even have kid-friendly distances and activities.

Festive Atmosphere: The event often features a lively and festive atmosphere, with music, entertainment, and cheering spectators along the race routes.

Awards and Prizes: Participants often have the chance to win awards or prizes based on their performance in the races, adding a competitive edge to the event.

Charitable Aspect: Some events, like charity runs or fundraisers, may have a charitable aspect, supporting local causes or organizations.

Health and Wellness Expo: The classic event may include a health and wellness expo where participants can learn about fitness, nutrition, and overall well-being.

Post-Race Celebrations: After completing the race, you can join in post-race celebrations, enjoy refreshments, and connect with fellow participants.

Costumes and Themes: Some races incorporate themes or encourage participants to wear costumes, adding an extra element of fun and creativity.

Scenic Beach Setting: The event's location on or near the beach provides a picturesque setting, making it an ideal backdrop for post-race relaxation and celebrations.

Attending the St. Pete Beach Classic is not only a chance to engage in physical activity and challenge yourself but also an opportunity to embrace the beach culture and community spirit of St. Pete Beach. Whether you're a seasoned runner, a beginner, or someone looking for a fun and festive outing, this classic event offers an enjoyable and memorable experience. Be sure to check the event's schedule, registration details, and any specific requirements or guidelines for participation.

84. Join a community beach cleanup event.

Participating in a community beach cleanup event in St. Petersburg, Florida is a wonderful way to contribute to the well-being of the local environment and connect with like-minded individuals who share a passion for preserving the coastline. Here's what you can expect when you join a beach cleanup event:

Environmental Impact: Beach cleanups help remove litter and debris from the shoreline, contributing to cleaner and safer beaches for both residents and wildlife.

Community Engagement: You'll have the opportunity to meet and connect with local residents who are passionate about environmental conservation, fostering a sense of community and shared responsibility.

Volunteer Effort: Beach cleanups are typically organized by volunteers or environmental organizations, and your participation is a valuable contribution to the cause.

Beach Access: Enjoy the beauty of the beach while actively participating in its preservation. It's a meaningful way to give back to the natural environment.

Educational Experience: Many beach cleanup events provide information about the local ecosystem, marine life, and the impact of pollution on the environment.

Equipment Provided: Organizers often supply trash bags, gloves, and other cleanup equipment. You simply need to bring your enthusiasm and willingness to help.

All Ages Welcome: Beach cleanups are family-friendly events, making them an ideal activity for individuals of all ages. It's an opportunity to teach children about environmental stewardship.

Group Effort: Cleaning the beach with a group makes the task more enjoyable and efficient. It's also a great team-building experience for corporate or school groups.

Environmental Awareness: Through participation, you become more aware of the environmental challenges faced by coastal communities and the importance of reducing litter and plastic waste.

Feel-Good Experience: Knowing that you've made a positive impact on the environment and the local community is a rewarding and fulfilling experience.

To join a beach cleanup event in St. Petersburg, keep an eye on local environmental organizations, volunteer groups, and community calendars for upcoming cleanup initiatives. You can also check with city or county parks and recreation departments, as they may organize or promote beach cleanup events in the area. By participating in these events, you'll play a part in preserving the natural beauty of St. Petersburg's coastal areas and ensuring they remain clean and enjoyable for all.

85. Take a historic preservation tour.

Taking a historic preservation tour in St. Petersburg, Florida, offers a unique opportunity to explore the city's rich history, architectural heritage, and cultural significance. Here's what you can expect when you participate in a historic preservation tour:

Guided Expertise: Tours are typically led by knowledgeable guides or historians who can provide insights into the historical significance of various landmarks, buildings, and districts.

Architectural Styles: Learn about the architectural styles that have influenced the city's development, from Mediterranean Revival and Art Deco to mid-century modern and Victorian architecture.

Historical Landmarks: Visit iconic historical landmarks, buildings, and neighborhoods that played a pivotal role in St. Petersburg's growth and development.

Cultural Context: Gain a deeper understanding of the cultural and social context of different eras in the city's history, from its founding to more recent developments.

Preservation Efforts: Explore the efforts made by local preservationists and organizations to protect and maintain historical structures and districts.

Stories and Anecdotes: Hear fascinating stories, anecdotes, and historical tidbits related to the places you visit, bringing the past to life.

Interactive Experience: Some tours may offer interactive elements, such as the opportunity to enter historic buildings, museums, or restored homes.

Walking or Trolley Tours: Tours may be conducted on foot, by trolley, or by other means of transportation, depending on the specific tour.

Group Experience: Enjoy the tour with like-minded individuals who share an interest in history and preservation, making it a great opportunity to connect with others.

Customization: Some tour operators offer customizable tours that cater to specific interests, such as architecture, art, or a particular historical era.

Educational Value: Historical preservation tours are not only informative but also educational, making them an ideal experience for students, history buffs, and those with a thirst for knowledge.

Appreciation of Heritage: By participating in these tours, you'll develop a deeper appreciation for the heritage and cultural significance of St. Petersburg.

The city may offer a range of themed tours, such as architectural tours, neighborhood walks, or even cemetery tours that provide a unique perspective on local history. Additionally, many tours can be tailored to specific areas of interest, ensuring a personalized and enriching experience. Be sure to research tour options, availability, and any associated fees to plan a tour that aligns with your historical interests.

86.Enjoy a round of mini-golf.

Enjoying a round of mini-golf in St. Petersburg, Florida, is a fun and family-friendly activity that offers a break from the ordinary and a chance to test your putting skills. Here's what you can expect when you indulge in a game of mini-golf:

Lively Atmosphere: Mini-golf courses are typically designed with creative and often whimsical themes, creating an enjoyable and vibrant environment for players of all ages.

Challenging Holes: Mini-golf courses feature a variety of challenging holes with obstacles like windmills, tunnels, water hazards, and more, making the game both entertaining and competitive.

Family Fun: Mini-golf is an ideal activity for families, allowing children and adults to participate together and have a great time.

Group or Date Night: Whether you're out with friends or on a date, mini-golf is a social and engaging pastime that promotes friendly competition.

Tournaments and Events: Some mini-golf venues host tournaments and special events that add an extra layer of excitement to the game.

Concessions and Snacks: Many mini-golf courses have on-site concessions or snack bars where you can grab a refreshment or a quick bite to eat.

Nighttime Golf: Some courses offer nighttime mini-golf with creative lighting and glow-in-the-dark features for a unique and entertaining experience.

Accessible for All Ages: Mini-golf is accessible to players of all skill levels, so everyone can participate and have a good time.

Affordable Entertainment: Mini-golf is often an affordable and budget-friendly entertainment option for both locals and tourists.

Themed Courses: Explore mini-golf courses with various themes, such as pirate adventures, tropical paradises, or even historic settings.

Skill Improvement: Mini-golf can be a great way to improve your putting skills, which can be beneficial if you're a golf enthusiast.

Party and Event Venue: Mini-golf courses often serve as unique venues for birthday parties, corporate events, and other gatherings.

To enjoy a round of mini-golf in St. Petersburg, you can search for local mini-golf courses, family entertainment centers, or themed mini-golf venues in the area. St. Petersburg and its surrounding areas likely offer a variety of options to choose from, so you can select a course that matches your preferences and theme.

87. Visit the Sunken Gardens for a yoga class.

Visiting Sunken Gardens for a yoga class is a fantastic way to combine the serenity of a historic botanical garden with the benefits of yoga practice. Here's what you can expect when you attend a yoga class in this beautiful garden:

Scenic Beauty: Sunken Gardens is renowned for its lush and serene environment, which provides a picturesque backdrop for yoga practice. Practicing yoga amidst the garden's greenery and blooming flowers is a truly peaceful experience.

Tranquil Atmosphere: The garden's peaceful ambiance offers an ideal setting for relaxation, meditation, and connecting with nature during your yoga session.

Professional Instructors: Yoga classes are typically led by experienced and certified yoga instructors who guide participants through various poses and techniques suitable for all skill levels.

Group Practice: Engage in a group yoga session, fostering a sense of community and shared wellness with fellow participants.

All Skill Levels: Classes often cater to individuals of all skill levels, from beginners to more advanced practitioners.

Mind-Body Connection: Yoga encourages the integration of physical postures, breathing techniques, and mindfulness, promoting a harmonious connection between the mind and body.

Health and Wellness: Yoga is known for its many health benefits, including improved flexibility, reduced stress, enhanced relaxation, and increased overall well-being.

Outdoor Experience: Practicing yoga outdoors amidst the garden's natural beauty allows you to absorb the fresh air and vitamin D from the sun.

Peaceful Reflection: After the yoga class, take time to stroll through Sunken Gardens and reflect on your practice while surrounded by the garden's serene landscapes.

Variety of Classes: Some venues may offer different types of yoga classes, such as Hatha, Vinyasa, or restorative yoga, allowing you to choose the style that suits your preferences.

To participate in a yoga class at Sunken Gardens, check their official website, contact them directly, or inquire with local yoga studios that may host classes in this picturesque setting. Make sure to confirm class schedules, any registration or fees, as well as any necessary equipment or attire to bring with you. Enjoy a tranquil and rejuvenating yoga experience amidst the natural beauty of Sunken Gardens in St. Petersburg.

88.Explore the Grand Central District for shopping.

Exploring the Grand Central District in St. Petersburg, Florida, for shopping is a delightful experience that offers a wide range of boutiques, galleries, and shops, as well as an opportunity to support local businesses. Here's what you can expect when you venture out for shopping in the Grand Central District:

Unique Boutiques: The Grand Central District is known for its eclectic boutiques that offer a diverse selection of clothing, accessories, home decor, and gifts. You'll find items that are often one-of-a-kind and have a distinctive local flair.

Art Galleries: Explore art galleries that showcase the work of talented local artists. You may have the chance to purchase original art pieces, sculptures, and unique art-related items.

Antiques and Vintage Finds: The district is home to antique shops and vintage stores where you can browse for collectibles, retro fashion, and timeless treasures.

Local Craft Shops: Support local artisans by visiting craft shops that feature handmade jewelry, pottery, and other artisanal products.

Cafes and Eateries: Many of the shops in the Grand Central District are situated near cafes and eateries. Enjoy a coffee, lunch, or a sweet treat during your shopping excursion.

Quaint Bookstores: If you're a book lover, keep an eye out for independent bookstores that offer a diverse range of titles and cozy reading nooks.

Farmers' Markets: Depending on the day and time of your visit, you might come across local farmers' markets with fresh produce, artisan foods, and handmade goods.

Local Flavors: Discover specialty shops that sell locally produced items, including gourmet foods, spices, and beverages that offer a taste of the region.

Charming Atmosphere: The district boasts a charming and pedestrian-friendly atmosphere, making it an enjoyable place for leisurely strolls and exploration.

Community Engagement: By shopping in the Grand Central District, you'll be supporting the local community and contributing to the vibrant economy of the area.

Special Events: Keep an eye on the district's event calendar, as there are often special shopping events, art walks, and festivals that offer even more reasons to visit.

Artistic Displays: Enjoy public art installations, murals, and creative displays that enhance the visual appeal of the district.

When shopping in the Grand Central District, you'll discover a variety of hidden gems and unique finds that cater to various tastes and interests. Whether you're in search of fashion, art, vintage items, or souvenirs to commemorate your visit to St. Petersburg, this district is sure to have something special for you. Be sure to check the opening hours of individual shops and any special events or promotions that might coincide with your visit.

89. Attend the St. Petersburg Second Saturday ArtWalk.

Attending the St. Petersburg Second Saturday ArtWalk is a vibrant and culturally enriching experience that allows you to explore the city's thriving art scene. Here's what you can expect when you participate in this monthly art event:

Art Galleries: The ArtWalk typically includes a wide range of art galleries, studios, and exhibition spaces that feature diverse works of art, including paintings, sculptures, photography, and more.

Local Artists: Meet and interact with local artists, many of whom may be present during the event to discuss their work, share their creative process, and answer questions.

Artistic Diversity: The ArtWalk showcases a variety of artistic styles and genres, making it an excellent opportunity to discover new and established talents.

Gallery Openings: Some galleries may use the ArtWalk as an occasion to unveil new exhibitions or hold opening receptions for artists, allowing you to be among the first to view their work.

Live Demonstrations: Witness live art demonstrations, such as painting or sculpting, giving you insight into the artistic process.

Performance Art: In addition to visual art, the ArtWalk may include performance art, music, dance, or other live entertainment.

Local Businesses: Explore shops and businesses in the area that participate in the ArtWalk and may feature art-related displays or host special events.

Food and Drink: Many galleries and venues provide refreshments or partner with local restaurants and cafes, creating a delightful atmosphere for food and beverage enthusiasts.

Cultural Experience: Immerse yourself in the local culture and artistic heritage of St. Petersburg while supporting the creative community.

Networking: The event offers an opportunity to connect with fellow art enthusiasts, artists, and collectors, fostering a sense of community and appreciation for the arts.

Art Purchases: If you find a piece of art that resonates with you, the ArtWalk provides the opportunity to purchase artwork directly from the artists or galleries.

Family-Friendly: The ArtWalk is often family-friendly, making it a suitable outing for all ages. It's an opportunity to introduce children to the world of art and creativity.

The St. Petersburg Second Saturday ArtWalk is a recurring event, so you can plan your visit for the second Saturday of each month. To make the most of your experience, check the event's official website or contact the local galleries and participating venues for maps, schedules, and additional information. Don't forget to take your time, soak in the artistic ambiance, and appreciate the talent and creativity on display during this celebration of art and culture in St. Petersburg.

90.Take a Segway tour of the city.

Taking a Segway tour of St. Petersburg, Florida, is a fun and unique way to explore the city's attractions and learn about its history and culture. Here's what you can expect when you embark on a Segway tour:

Easy and Fun Riding: Riding a Segway is easy to learn and enjoyable. Most tour operators provide a brief training session to ensure that you're comfortable and confident before you start.

Travel to St. Petersburg Florida

Expert Guide: Segway tours are led by knowledgeable and entertaining guides who share interesting facts, historical anecdotes, and local insights about St. Petersburg as you glide through the city.

Scenic Routes: Explore scenic routes that take you to key landmarks, parks, and historic sites. You'll have the chance to see the city's highlights while covering more ground than you would on foot.

Cultural and Historical Stops: Segway tours often include stops at cultural and historical attractions, allowing you to delve into the city's heritage.

Photo Opportunities: Enjoy numerous photo opportunities along the way, including breathtaking views, public art, and architectural gems.

Group Experience: Segway tours are often enjoyed in small groups, creating a social and engaging experience as you get to know fellow participants.

Custom Tours: Some tour operators offer customizable tours, so you can focus on specific interests, such as art, history, or nature.

Safety and Equipment: Segway tours prioritize safety, providing participants with helmets and ensuring that the equipment is well-maintained.

Environmental Awareness: Riding a Segway is an eco-friendly mode of transportation, aligning with St. Petersburg's commitment to sustainability.

Unique Perspective: The elevated view from a Segway allows you to see the city from a unique perspective, making it easier to appreciate its beauty and architecture.

Cover More Ground: With a Segway, you can explore a wider area in a shorter amount of time, making it an efficient way to see the city's top attractions.

All Skill Levels: Segway tours are suitable for participants of all ages and fitness levels, making them accessible to a wide range of people.

To experience a Segway tour of St. Petersburg, you can look for local tour operators that offer guided Segway excursions. Be sure to check tour schedules, duration, rates, and any age or weight restrictions that may apply. Riding a Segway is a memorable and enjoyable way to discover the beauty and culture of St. Petersburg, and it's an adventure that many visitors find both educational and entertaining.

91.Experience a dolphin encounter program at the Clearwater Marine Aquarium.

Experiencing a dolphin encounter program at the Clearwater Marine Aquarium is a unique and memorable opportunity to get up close and personal with these intelligent and playful marine animals. As of my last knowledge update in January 2022, the Clearwater Marine Aquarium offered various programs that allowed visitors to engage with dolphins, including their famous resident, Winter, the bottlenose dolphin featured in the "Dolphin Tale" movies. Here's what you can typically expect from a dolphin encounter program at the Clearwater Marine Aquarium:

Educational Sessions: Dolphin encounter programs often begin with an informative orientation or presentation about the aquarium's marine mammal conservation efforts, dolphin biology, behavior, and the importance of protecting marine life.

Meet the Dolphins: You'll have the chance to meet and interact with dolphins like Winter, Hope, and others. These dolphins are often rescue animals that have been rehabilitated and cannot be released back into the wild.

Observation and Interaction: Depending on the program, you may observe the dolphins in their habitat, learn about their training, and even participate in interactive sessions. These can include feeding, enrichment activities, and potentially hands-on experiences.

Professional Guidance: Knowledgeable trainers and staff guide you through the experience, ensuring safety and providing insights into the dolphins' personalities and behaviors.

Photo Opportunities: Capture unforgettable moments with the dolphins, whether it's a photo with these amazing creatures or observing their acrobatics and behaviors up close.

Marine Conservation Education: Learn about the importance of marine conservation, the challenges facing dolphins and other marine life, and what you can do to help protect the oceans.

Hands-On Experience: Some programs may offer opportunities for more hands-on interaction, such as petting or feeding the dolphins, and educational encounters.

Memorabilia: Typically, you can purchase souvenirs or memorabilia related to your dolphin encounter, allowing you to take home a memento of your experience.

Please note that the availability and specifics of dolphin encounter programs can change, so it's essential to check the official website of the Clearwater Marine Aquarium or contact them directly for the most up-to-date information on program options, availability, schedules, and pricing. Additionally, due to the conservation focus of many marine facilities, these programs often have a strong educational component, emphasizing the importance of protecting marine life and their natural habitats. A dolphin encounter program can be an unforgettable and educational experience for anyone interested in marine life and the conservation of these magnificent creatures.

92.Visit Tampa Bay Watch Discovery Center.

Visiting the Tampa Bay Watch Discovery Center is a fantastic way to learn about and connect with the unique and diverse marine ecosystems of the Tampa Bay area. Here's what you can expect when you explore this educational and environmental center:

Educational Exhibits: The Discovery Center typically features a range of informative exhibits that provide insights into the ecosystems, wildlife, and environmental challenges of Tampa Bay and the Gulf of Mexico.

Marine Life: Learn about the diverse marine life that inhabits Tampa Bay, including fish, birds, mammals, and other aquatic species. Interactive displays and aquariums may offer a close look at local creatures.

Environmental Conservation: Discover the vital conservation efforts and initiatives undertaken by Tampa Bay Watch to protect and restore the delicate balance of the bay's ecosystems.

Hands-On Activities: Many environmental centers offer hands-on activities for visitors of all ages, allowing you to engage with marine life, explore touch tanks, or participate in interactive learning experiences.

Educational Programs: The center may host educational programs, workshops, and events that focus on various aspects of marine and environmental science. These may include guided nature walks, bird watching, and marine clean-up initiatives.

Nature Trails: Some centers have nearby nature trails or boardwalks that lead to the bay, providing opportunities for wildlife observation and exploration.

Expert Guides: Knowledgeable staff and volunteers are often available to answer questions, share insights, and provide guided tours of the center's exhibits and nearby natural areas.

Marine and Environmental Education: The Discovery Center is often dedicated to educating visitors about the significance of preserving the bay's ecosystems and the ways in which individuals can contribute to environmental conservation.

Scenic Views: Many centers are located in picturesque settings with beautiful waterfront views, providing a serene and inspiring backdrop for your visit.

Community Engagement: By visiting the Discovery Center, you support local organizations that are committed to protecting and preserving Tampa Bay's unique natural resources.

To get the most up-to-date information about the Tampa Bay Watch Discovery Center's exhibits, programs, hours of operation, and visitor guidelines, I recommend checking their official website or contacting them directly. Your visit to the Discovery Center offers a chance to gain a deeper understanding of the importance of environmental stewardship and the remarkable ecosystems of Tampa Bay.

93.Explore Tampa Bay's islands by ferry.

Exploring Tampa Bay's islands by ferry is a delightful way to experience the natural beauty, diverse ecosystems, and unique island destinations that the Tampa Bay area has to offer. Here's what you can typically expect when you embark on a ferry adventure to the islands of Tampa Bay:

Travel to St. Petersburg Florida

Scenic Cruises: Enjoy scenic ferry rides that provide stunning views of the bay, local wildlife, and the surrounding coastal landscapes.

Island Destinations: Ferry services often connect to a variety of islands in the Tampa Bay area, each with its own distinct features and attractions.

Nature and Wildlife: Explore the natural beauty of the islands, including pristine beaches, lush vegetation, and opportunities for wildlife watching.

Outdoor Activities: Many islands offer outdoor activities such as hiking, picnicking, kayaking, and snorkeling, making them ideal for nature enthusiasts and adventurers.

Historical Sites: Some islands are home to historical sites, including lighthouses, forts, and remnants of early settlements, providing insights into the region's history.

Dining and Refreshments: Depending on the island, you may find restaurants, cafes, and snack bars where you can enjoy a meal or refreshments.

Cultural Events: Some islands host cultural events, festivals, or educational programs that offer a deeper understanding of the local culture and heritage.

Relaxation and Beach Time: Many ferry destinations boast pristine and less crowded beaches, making them perfect for relaxation, sunbathing, and swimming.

Community Engagement: By taking a ferry to the islands, you're often contributing to the local economy and supporting island communities.

Customizable Itineraries: Depending on the ferry service, you can customize your itinerary to visit specific islands and spend as much time as you like exploring each one.

Guided Tours: Some ferry operators offer guided tours that provide information about the islands' history, ecology, and points of interest.

Environmental Awareness: Ferry services may emphasize the importance of environmental conservation and sustainable tourism practices.

The islands of Tampa Bay, including places like Egmont Key, Caladesi Island, and Honeymoon Island, offer a range of experiences, from pristine natural settings to recreational activities and historical sites. To plan your island-hopping adventure, check with local ferry operators for schedules, routes, ticket prices, and any additional information about each island's offerings. Whether you're interested in exploring the great outdoors, relaxing on unspoiled beaches, or delving into local history, Tampa Bay's islands by ferry provide a diverse array of experiences for all types of travelers.

94. Take a scenic drive along the Gulf of Mexico.

Taking a scenic drive along the Gulf of Mexico in the Tampa Bay area is a breathtaking way to experience the region's stunning coastal beauty. Here's how you can enjoy a memorable coastal drive:

Route Selection: Choose a scenic route that hugs the Gulf of Mexico coastline. Some of the most picturesque drives in the area include the Gulf Boulevard in St. Pete Beach, the Fort De Soto Park Causeway, or the drive along the shoreline of Clearwater Beach.

Coastal Vistas: As you drive, you'll be treated to breathtaking views of the Gulf's turquoise waters and the pristine, sandy beaches that line the coast. Keep your camera handy for plenty of photo opportunities.

Sunsets: The Gulf Coast is renowned for its stunning sunsets. Consider planning your drive in the late afternoon to catch a memorable sunset over the water.

Beach Stops: Along the way, you can stop at various beach access points to take a stroll on the sand, dip your toes in the water, or simply relax while listening to the soothing sound of the waves.

State Parks and Nature Reserves: Explore the natural beauty of the area by visiting state parks and nature reserves like Fort De Soto Park, which offer hiking trails, birdwatching, and opportunities to connect with local wildlife.

Coastal Dining: Many charming coastal towns and beach communities along the drive offer a variety of seaside restaurants and seafood shacks where you can savor fresh seafood and enjoy Gulf views.

Water Sports: If you're an adventurous traveler, you may find opportunities for water sports like kayaking, paddleboarding, and parasailing at various stops along the drive.

Historical Sites: Learn about the history of the Gulf Coast by visiting local historical sites and landmarks, such as the Fort De Soto Historic Fort or the Clearwater Beach Walk.

Art and Culture: The Gulf Coast has a thriving arts and cultural scene. Explore local art galleries and museums that showcase the work of regional artists.

Shelling: The Gulf's gentle waves often deliver beautiful seashells to the shore. Don't forget to search for seashells or even participate in shelling excursions if they are available.

Local Events: Check for any local events or festivals happening along the coast, as these can add a unique cultural experience to your drive.

Biking and Walking Trails: Many coastal communities offer scenic biking and walking paths along the shoreline, so consider bringing your bicycle or going for a leisurely walk.

Whether you're planning a leisurely drive or a more adventurous exploration of the Gulf Coast, a scenic drive along the Gulf of Mexico is an excellent way to appreciate the region's natural beauty, coastal charm, and the soothing sound of the waves. It's a journey that offers relaxation, outdoor activities, and opportunities to immerse yourself in the Gulf's serene ambiance.

95.Discover the history of St. Petersburg through local historic districts.

Exploring the history of St. Petersburg through its local historic districts is a fascinating journey that offers insights into the city's development, architecture, and cultural heritage. St. Petersburg boasts several historic districts, each with its own unique character and stories to tell. Here are some of the historic districts you can explore to learn about the history of St. Petersburg:

Old Northeast: Located near downtown St. Petersburg, the Old Northeast neighborhood features beautiful historic homes from the early 20th century.

Take a stroll through the brick-paved streets and admire the architectural styles, including Mediterranean Revival, Craftsman, and Colonial Revival.

Historic Kenwood: Known for its bungalow-style homes, Historic Kenwood is an art and craftsman district. The area hosts the annual "BungalowFest" event, allowing you to tour these charming and historically significant homes.

Granada Terrace: This neighborhood features Mediterranean Revival architecture and beautiful homes from the 1920s. The historic Coliseum Ballroom and Mirror Lake Shuffleboard Club are nearby.

Driftwood: The Driftwood neighborhood is recognized for its unique "birdcage" homes, designed to protect against mosquitoes. It's a testament to the innovative designs of the early 20th century.

Roser Park: Roser Park is one of the oldest neighborhoods in St. Petersburg, known for its historic bungalows, cobblestone streets, and lush landscaping.

Central Arts District: While primarily known for its arts scene, the Central Arts District is home to numerous historic buildings and murals that showcase the city's cultural history.

Downtown St. Petersburg: The heart of the city contains a blend of historic and modern structures. You'll find architectural gems like the Vinoy Hotel, which has a storied past, and the iconic St. Petersburg Shuffleboard Club.

Pasadena on the Gulf: Explore the history of the city's growth through the mid-20th century and the development of the Pasadena Golf Club Estates, which was one of the early residential areas in the region.

Lealman: Lealman is a historic neighborhood with a diverse history that includes the presence of citrus groves and the establishment of the Lealman and Kenwood neighborhoods, which have distinct histories.

Al Lang's St. Petersburg: Named after Mayor Al Lang, this area holds historical significance for its association with baseball and the St. Petersburg Devil Rays, and it's home to the famous Al Lang Stadium.

To explore these historic districts and learn more about the history of St. Petersburg, consider taking self-guided walking tours, visiting local historical societies or museums, or joining guided tours led by knowledgeable historians or tour guides. Each historic district offers a unique window into the past and showcases the architectural and cultural heritage of St. Petersburg, allowing you to connect with the city's rich history in a meaningful way.

96.Attend the St. Pete Folk Fair.

The St. Pete Folk Fair is an exciting annual event that celebrates folk music, arts, and culture in St. Petersburg, Florida. Attending the fair offers a unique opportunity to immerse yourself in the world of folk traditions and enjoy a diverse range of activities and performances. Here's what you can typically expect when you attend the St. Pete Folk Fair:

Live Music Performances: The heart of any folk fair is its music, and you can anticipate a wide variety of live folk music performances. These may include traditional folk songs, acoustic sets, and performances by local and regional folk musicians and bands.

Folk Arts and Crafts: Explore displays of folk arts and crafts, including handmade jewelry, textiles, pottery, woodwork, and other traditional crafts created by local artisans. It's an excellent opportunity to shop for unique, handcrafted items.

Dance and Demonstrations: Folk fairs often feature dance performances and demonstrations. You might see traditional folk dances, square dancing, clogging, or other forms of folk dance from different cultures.

Workshops and Educational Sessions: The fair may offer workshops and educational sessions on various folk traditions, including music, dance, and craft techniques. These can be an excellent way to learn more about different aspects of folk culture.

Food and Cuisine: Savor a variety of traditional folk foods and cuisine, such as regional dishes and international fare. Food stalls and food trucks often offer a wide selection of delicious options.

Local Artisans and Vendors: Local artisans and vendors typically set up booths to showcase and sell their folk-inspired creations. It's a great place to support local talent and discover unique items.

Interactive Activities: Folk fairs often include interactive activities for all ages, such as sing-alongs, jam sessions, storytelling, and hands-on craft activities.

Community and Cultural Exchange: Engage with the local community and enjoy the opportunity to connect with people who share an appreciation for folk traditions and culture.

Children's Activities: Many folk fairs are family-friendly and offer children's activities, games, and entertainment to keep the younger attendees engaged.

Cultural Diversity: Folk fairs celebrate the rich tapestry of cultural diversity, providing a platform to learn about and appreciate different traditions and customs.

Community Performances: Some folk fairs include community performances by local schools, community groups, and folk clubs, adding to the festive atmosphere.

Live Storytelling: Immerse yourself in the art of storytelling with live performances that share folk tales and stories from various cultures.

To attend the St. Pete Folk Fair, check the event's official website or social media pages for the latest information on dates, location, admission, and a schedule of performances and activities. It's a wonderful opportunity to enjoy the sights, sounds, and tastes of folk culture while connecting with the local community in St. Petersburg.

97.Explore local vintage shops and boutiques.

Exploring local vintage shops and boutiques in St. Petersburg, Florida, is a fantastic way to discover unique treasures, antiques, retro fashion, and one-of-a-kind items. St. Petersburg has a vibrant vintage shopping scene, and you'll find a variety of shops and boutiques to explore. Here's how to make the most of your vintage shopping experience:

Central Avenue: Start your vintage shopping adventure on Central Avenue, which is known for its eclectic mix of shops, including vintage boutiques, thrift stores, and antique shops. This area is a hub for retro fashion and collectibles.

Travel to St. Petersburg Florida

Grand Central District: The Grand Central District is home to a range of vintage shops and antique stores. It's an ideal place to browse for unique clothing, home decor, and other vintage items.

Beach Drive: If you're interested in high-end vintage and designer consignment, head to the upscale boutiques on Beach Drive. You might find vintage fashion and accessories from renowned brands.

Thrift Stores: St. Petersburg has numerous thrift stores where you can hunt for affordable vintage clothing and home goods. Some popular options include Goodwill, Salvation Army, and local thrift shops.

Antique Stores: Explore antique stores that specialize in furniture, collectibles, and unique decor pieces. These stores often have a wide range of items from different eras.

Vintage Clothing Shops: For vintage fashion enthusiasts, look for specialized vintage clothing stores that offer clothing, accessories, and footwear from various decades.

Retro and Mid-Century Modern: If you're a fan of mid-century modern design, check out retro and vintage shops that focus on furniture, lighting, and decor from the mid-20th century.

Art and Collectibles: Some vintage shops in St. Petersburg specialize in vintage art, posters, vinyl records, and other collectibles.

Flea Markets and Pop-Up Markets: Keep an eye out for local flea markets and pop-up vintage markets, which often feature a wide variety of vendors and items. These events are a great way to discover hidden gems.

Local Artisan Boutiques: In addition to vintage shops, explore local artisan boutiques that offer handmade and artisanal products, including jewelry, pottery, and other crafts.

Local Flavor: Take the opportunity to meet the shop owners and chat with them about their curated collections. They can often provide valuable insights and history about the items they sell.

Check for Events: Keep an eye on local event calendars for vintage fairs, antique shows, and vintage clothing swaps, where you can interact with other vintage enthusiasts and sellers.

Before you embark on your vintage shopping adventure, it's a good idea to plan your route, check shop hours, and bring a list of items you're interested in finding. Vintage shopping can be a delightful and rewarding experience, whether you're looking to add unique pieces to your wardrobe, decorate your home with vintage charm, or simply enjoy the thrill of the hunt.

98.Discover the city's diverse culinary scene.

St. Petersburg, Florida, boasts a diverse culinary scene that reflects the city's cultural mix and vibrant atmosphere. Exploring the local restaurants and eateries is a delightful way to savor a wide range of flavors and cuisines. Here are some tips for discovering the city's diverse culinary scene:

Seafood: Given its coastal location, St. Petersburg is renowned for its fresh seafood. Enjoy dishes like grouper, shrimp, and crab prepared in various styles, from traditional fried to innovative gourmet presentations.

International Cuisine: Explore the city's international culinary offerings, from Cuban sandwiches to sushi, Thai, Vietnamese, and Ethiopian cuisine. St. Petersburg has a rich tapestry of international flavors.

Farm-to-Table: Discover farm-to-table restaurants that prioritize locally sourced, seasonal ingredients. These establishments offer dishes that reflect the flavors of the region.

Food Trucks and Street Food: Keep an eye out for food trucks and street food vendors, which often serve delicious, quick, and affordable options from various culinary traditions.

Southern Comfort Food: Experience the Southern comfort food scene with classics like fried chicken, biscuits and gravy, and grits. Enjoy soulful dishes at local diners and eateries.

Craft Breweries: Many craft breweries in St. Petersburg serve craft beer alongside gourmet pub fare. Pair local brews with dishes like artisanal burgers, fish tacos, and beer-infused cuisine.

Travel to St. Petersburg Florida

Vegetarian and Vegan Options: St. Petersburg is known for its vegetarian and vegan-friendly restaurants. Explore innovative plant-based dishes and delicious meatless alternatives.

Fine Dining: Treat yourself to fine dining at upscale restaurants in St. Petersburg, which often feature tasting menus, wine pairings, and top-tier service. These establishments are ideal for special occasions.

Bakeries and Cafes: Enjoy a leisurely breakfast or brunch at local cafes and bakeries that offer freshly baked pastries, artisan coffee, and gourmet sandwiches.

Waterfront Dining: Many restaurants in the area offer stunning waterfront views. Dining by the bay or Gulf of Mexico while enjoying a meal is a memorable experience.

Local Cuisine: Seek out local dishes and culinary traditions that are unique to the area. For example, try the famous Cuban sandwich, gulf-to-table oysters, or Florida's signature Key lime pie.

Food Tours: Join food tours in the city that guide you through a variety of culinary experiences, allowing you to sample a range of dishes and learn about their history.

Food and Arts Districts: Visit local food and arts districts, such as the EDGE District, which are known for their concentration of restaurants, cafes, and shops.

Live Music and Dining: Enjoy live music while dining at restaurants that feature local musicians and bands. It's a great way to savor dinner and entertainment simultaneously.

Local Markets: Attend local food markets or farmers' markets, where you can sample artisanal products and enjoy the community atmosphere.

To discover St. Petersburg's diverse culinary scene, research local restaurants and dining options in different neighborhoods, read reviews, and ask locals for recommendations. Whether you're a food enthusiast, an adventurous eater, or someone looking to explore new flavors, you'll find a wide array of dining experiences to savor in the city.

99.Experience St. Petersburg's nightlife at bars and clubs.

St. Petersburg, Florida, offers a vibrant and diverse nightlife scene with a variety of bars, clubs, and entertainment venues to enjoy after the sun sets. Whether you're into live music, craft cocktails, dancing, or just unwinding with friends, St. Petersburg has something for everyone. Here's how to experience the city's nightlife:

Downtown St. Pete: The heart of the city is home to numerous bars and clubs. Central Avenue and Beach Drive are hotspots for nightlife, with a range of bars, clubs, and lounges to explore.

Craft Breweries: St. Petersburg has a thriving craft beer scene. Visit local breweries that offer a wide selection of craft beers, live music, and often, food trucks.

Live Music Venues: Discover live music at venues like Jannus Live, The Palladium Theater, and Ruby's Elixir, which host local and touring bands, covering a variety of musical genres.

Dance Clubs: Dance the night away at clubs featuring DJs and dance floors. Some clubs offer different music styles, from electronic and hip-hop to Latin and reggae.

Rooftop Bars: Enjoy beautiful views of the city and waterfront from rooftop bars. These venues often offer specialty cocktails and a trendy atmosphere.

Sports Bars: If you're a sports enthusiast, visit sports bars with large screens to catch your favorite games, along with pub grub and drinks.

Cocktail Bars: Sip on craft cocktails at upscale cocktail bars, where mixologists create unique and artisanal drinks.

Karaoke Bars: Sing your heart out at karaoke bars that provide a lively and entertaining atmosphere.

Gay Bars and LGBTQ+ Clubs: St. Petersburg has a welcoming LGBTQ+ scene with bars and clubs that cater to the community and allies.

Late-Night Eats: Look for bars and restaurants that serve late-night snacks and comfort food, making for the perfect post-drinks meal.

Themed Nights: Some bars and clubs host themed nights or special events, such as '80s dance parties, salsa nights, and trivia nights.

Jazz Clubs: Discover intimate jazz clubs where you can enjoy live jazz performances while sipping on cocktails.

Art and Culture: Combine art and nightlife by visiting galleries that host evening art events and openings with live music and refreshments.

Hookah Lounges: Experience the flavors of hookah at hookah lounges, often with a Middle Eastern ambiance and a variety of shisha options.

Waterfront Dining: Some restaurants and bars along the waterfront offer an ideal setting to enjoy drinks and a picturesque view of the water.

Remember to check the hours of operation, event schedules, and dress codes for specific venues before heading out. Whether you're seeking a laid-back evening with friends, dancing until dawn, or enjoying live performances, St. Petersburg's nightlife scene has something for everyone to savor the night in style.

100.Join a craft beer tour to sample local brews.

Joining a craft beer tour in St. Petersburg is a fantastic way to explore the city's thriving craft beer scene and sample a variety of local brews. Craft beer tours typically provide a guided and curated experience, allowing you to learn about the brewing process, discover unique flavors, and connect with the local beer community. Here's how to make the most of a craft beer tour in St. Petersburg:

Research and Choose a Tour: Start by researching craft beer tour options in St. Petersburg. Look for tours that align with your interests, whether you're into hoppy IPAs, barrel-aged stouts, or experimental brews. You can find walking tours, bus tours, and brewery hopping options.

Local Breweries: St. Petersburg is home to a growing number of craft breweries, each with its own distinct personality and offerings. Check which breweries are included in the tour and if they match your beer preferences.

Guided Tastings: Craft beer tours often include guided tastings at each brewery. You'll have the chance to sample a flight of different beers, from lagers and ales to sours and porters. Take notes and ask questions about the brewing process.

Brewery Tours: Most craft beer tours incorporate brewery tours. These behind-the-scenes experiences provide insights into the brewing process, from mashing and fermenting to bottling and kegging.

Meet Brewmasters: On some tours, you might meet the brewmasters and hear about the history of the breweries and their approach to craft beer.

Local Insights: Craft beer tours often feature knowledgeable guides who share local insights about the beer scene, the city's history, and the breweries' stories.

Food Pairings: Some tours include food pairings, allowing you to enjoy the synergy of beer and cuisine. Beer and cheese pairings, beer and barbecue, or beer and charcuterie are popular options.

Transportation: Depending on the tour, transportation may be provided. It could be a walking tour within a specific neighborhood, a bus tour to multiple breweries, or even a boat tour if you want a unique experience.

Souvenirs: Look for tours that offer souvenirs, such as branded glassware or merchandise from the breweries you visit.

Responsible Drinking: Enjoy the tour responsibly, and be sure to pace yourself. Drinking water between samples can help maintain your palate and ensure you have an enjoyable experience.

Plan Ahead: Make reservations for the craft beer tour in advance, as they can fill up quickly, especially on weekends.

Support Local: Remember that by participating in craft beer tours, you're supporting local breweries and the craft beer community in St. Petersburg.

Craft beer tours provide a fun and educational way to immerse yourself in the local beer culture, meet fellow beer enthusiasts, and explore the city's neighborhoods. Whether you're a craft beer connoisseur or just looking to try something new, these tours offer a taste of St. Petersburg's evolving craft beer landscape.

101.Go wine tasting at local wineries.

While St. Petersburg, Florida, is more famous for its craft breweries and beachfront bars, you can still enjoy wine tasting at local wineries in the surrounding region. The climate in the Tampa Bay area is not as conducive to winemaking as traditional wine regions, but some wineries produce unique Florida wines and offer tasting experiences. Here's how to go wine tasting at local wineries near St. Petersburg:

Lakeridge Winery & Vineyards: Located in Clermont, about a two-hour drive from St. Petersburg, Lakeridge Winery is one of the largest and most well-known wineries in Florida. They produce a range of wines, including muscadine, and offer complimentary tours and tastings. The winery often hosts events and festivals.

Keel & Curley Winery: Located in Plant City, roughly an hour's drive from St. Petersburg, Keel & Curley Winery specializes in blueberry wines and offers tastings of their fruit wines. They also have a tasting room and events like "U-Pick" blueberry picking.

Florida Orange Groves Winery: Located in St. Petersburg itself, this winery produces a variety of tropical and citrus fruit wines, such as orange, key lime, and mango. You can visit their tasting room in the heart of St. Petersburg for a unique Florida wine experience.

Murielle Winery: Located in Clearwater, near St. Petersburg, Murielle Winery is a boutique winery that focuses on fruit and grape wines. They offer tastings and tours of their winemaking process.

Henscratch Farms Vineyard and Winery: While it's a bit farther away in Lake Placid (about a 2.5-hour drive), this winery offers a rustic and charming atmosphere for wine tastings and often hosts events like wine and art nights.

Wine Festivals: Keep an eye out for wine festivals and events in the Tampa Bay area. These festivals often feature multiple wineries and offer a great opportunity to sample various wines.

Before planning your visit, check the wineries' websites or contact them to confirm their hours of operation, tasting fees, and any special events. While wine production in Florida may not rival more traditional wine regions, the local wineries offer a unique taste of the state's fruity and tropical wines, which can be a delightful and refreshing experience.

102.Enjoy a rooftop dinner with a view.

A rooftop dinner with a view is a wonderful way to experience St. Petersburg's nightlife and take in the city's picturesque scenery. Several rooftop restaurants and bars in the area offer spectacular views of the city and the waterfront. Here's how to enjoy a memorable rooftop dinner in St. Petersburg:

Research Rooftop Venues: Start by researching rooftop restaurants and bars in St. Petersburg. Look for establishments that offer the ambiance, cuisine, and view you desire.

Reservations: Rooftop venues can be popular, so make a reservation in advance to secure your spot, especially if you plan to dine during peak hours or on special occasions.

Dress Code: Check the dress code for the venue you plan to visit. Some rooftop restaurants may have a smart-casual or dressier dress code, so dress appropriately.

Arrive Early for Sunset: If you want to enjoy a beautiful sunset while dining, plan to arrive early to secure a table with a view. Sunsets over the water are particularly stunning in St. Petersburg.

Cuisine Preferences: Choose a rooftop venue that offers cuisine that suits your tastes. Whether you're in the mood for seafood, international dishes, or American classics, you can find a rooftop restaurant to fit your preferences.

Craft Cocktails: Many rooftop bars have creative mixologists who craft unique and delicious cocktails. Take advantage of this and try a signature drink.

Live Music: Some rooftop venues feature live music or DJs. Check if the venue has any entertainment options during your visit.

Celebrate Special Occasions: Rooftop dinners are perfect for celebrating special occasions like anniversaries, birthdays, or romantic date nights.

Outdoor Seating: Most rooftop venues offer outdoor seating to fully enjoy the view and the fresh air. Make sure to check the weather forecast and dress accordingly.

Photography: Don't forget your camera or smartphone to capture the beautiful views and your memorable dining experience.

Local Recommendations: Ask locals or hotel staff for rooftop dining recommendations, as they might know hidden gems that aren't as well-known to tourists.

Some popular rooftop venues in St. Petersburg include The Canopy at The Birchwood, 360 Rooftop at Hotel Zamora, and Paul's Landing at The Vinoy Renaissance St. Petersburg Resort & Golf Club. Each of these venues offers a unique atmosphere and stunning vistas of the city and the waterfront.

Remember that rooftop dining is in high demand, so making a reservation is often the key to securing a table with the best view. Enjoy your rooftop dinner with a view and make it a memorable part of your St. Petersburg experience.

103.Attend a waterfront festival at Vinoy Park.

Vinoy Park is a picturesque waterfront park in St. Petersburg, Florida, known for hosting a variety of events and festivals throughout the year. Attending a waterfront festival at Vinoy Park is a fantastic way to enjoy the beautiful scenery, partake in local culture, and experience the city's vibrant atmosphere. Here's how to make the most of a festival at Vinoy Park:

Check the Event Calendar: Keep an eye on the event calendar for Vinoy Park to stay updated on upcoming festivals and activities. Events vary throughout the year and may include music festivals, art fairs, food festivals, and more.

Purchase Tickets: Some festivals may require tickets for admission, so it's a good idea to purchase them in advance to secure your spot. Check the event's website or local ticket vendors for details.

Plan Your Arrival: Consider arriving early to ensure you have ample time to explore the festival grounds, find parking, and choose a comfortable spot to enjoy the festivities.

Pack Essentials: Bring essentials like sunscreen, comfortable clothing, and a hat to protect yourself from the sun, especially if it's an outdoor event. Don't forget your smartphone or camera to capture the moments.

Enjoy Food and Drinks: Festivals often feature a variety of food vendors, so be sure to sample local cuisine and refreshments. You can savor regional dishes, international flavors, and sweet treats.

Live Entertainment: Many festivals at Vinoy Park offer live entertainment, including music performances, dance shows, and cultural displays. Check the festival lineup and schedule in advance to see what's in store.

Arts and Crafts: Explore arts and crafts booths to discover unique handmade items and support local artisans. You might find jewelry, clothing, pottery, and more.

Family-Friendly Activities: If you're attending with family, look for kid-friendly activities such as face painting, games, and interactive displays designed for children.

Community Engagement: Interact with local community organizations and learn more about the area's culture, history, and charitable causes.

Enjoy the View: Take in the stunning views of the waterfront and the surrounding area, including the Vinoy Renaissance St. Petersburg Resort & Golf Club.

Dance and Celebrate: Don't be shy about joining in the festivities. If there's music and dancing, take part in the celebration and have fun with fellow attendees.

Stay Hydrated: Florida's warm climate can make outdoor festivals quite hot. Stay hydrated by drinking plenty of water throughout the event.

Connect with Locals: Strike up conversations with local residents to learn more about St. Petersburg and gather tips for your stay.

Vinoy Park is a popular venue for a variety of festivals and events, so it's worth checking the schedule in advance to see what's happening during your visit. Whether you're interested in music, art, food, or culture, attending a festival at

Vinoy Park provides a great way to immerse yourself in the local scene and create lasting memories of your time in St. Petersburg.

104.Explore the history of Sunken Gardens.

Sunken Gardens is a historic botanical garden in St. Petersburg, Florida, known for its lush tropical landscapes, colorful flora, and serene atmosphere. It has a rich history that dates back to the early 20th century. Here's an overview of the history of Sunken Gardens:

Early Beginnings: Sunken Gardens was originally established in 1903 by George Turner, Sr. He purchased the land and began transforming it into a tropical garden. George Turner, Sr. was inspired by the idea of creating a "sunken" garden where visitors could escape the Florida heat and immerse themselves in a tranquil oasis.

Development and Expansion: Over the years, George Turner, Sr. expanded the garden, collecting and planting exotic plants from around the world. He created pools, meandering paths, and shaded areas, making it a haven for visitors and a home to an incredible variety of plant species.

The Turner Family: The Turner family, particularly George Turner, Jr., continued to maintain and enhance the gardens over the decades. They introduced features like flamingos, macaws, and other birds to add to the garden's allure.

St. Petersburg's First Tourist Attraction: Sunken Gardens became St. Petersburg's first major tourist attraction, drawing visitors from near and far. It was celebrated for its lush vegetation, cascading waterfalls, and its tranquil, sunken setting.

Challenges and Preservation: In the late 20th century, the gardens faced economic challenges and the threat of development. Concerned citizens and local leaders rallied to preserve this botanical gem. The city of St. Petersburg eventually purchased the gardens in 1999 to protect it from potential commercial development.

Listed on the National Register of Historic Places: In 2003, Sunken Gardens was added to the National Register of Historic Places, recognizing its cultural and historical significance in the community.

Continued Operation: Today, Sunken Gardens remains open to the public as a peaceful and educational attraction. Visitors can explore the winding paths, admire the diverse plant life, and attend events and educational programs held within the gardens.

Sunken Gardens is a testament to the enduring beauty of nature and the efforts of dedicated individuals to preserve a historical and horticultural treasure. It continues to be a place of relaxation, education, and natural beauty for residents and visitors to St. Petersburg.

105.Take a historic walking tour.

Taking a historic walking tour in St. Petersburg, Florida, is an excellent way to immerse yourself in the city's rich history, explore its architectural heritage, and learn about key landmarks and cultural sites. Here's how to make the most of your historic walking tour:

Select a Tour: St. Petersburg offers various historic walking tours led by knowledgeable guides. Research available tours to choose one that aligns with your interests, whether it's focused on the city's general history, a particular neighborhood, or a specific aspect of its heritage.

Tour Options: Consider tours that cover topics like the city's founding, architectural styles, local legends, and notable figures in St. Petersburg's history.

Schedule and Reservations: Check the tour's schedule and make reservations in advance. Some tours might have limited space, so booking early ensures you secure your spot.

Comfortable Footwear: Wear comfortable walking shoes and dress appropriately for the weather, as tours usually operate rain or shine.

Arrive Early: Arrive at the meeting point a little early to check in and ensure you don't miss the beginning of the tour.

Listen and Ask Questions: Pay close attention to your tour guide's narration, and don't hesitate to ask questions. Guides often share fascinating anecdotes and local knowledge.

Photography: Bring a camera or smartphone to capture photos of historic landmarks and points of interest along the way.

Water and Sunscreen: Especially in Florida's sunny climate, bring water and apply sunscreen to stay comfortable during the tour.

Rest Stops: Some tours include rest stops at local cafes or parks, so you can enjoy refreshments or sit down for a break.

Group Size: Be aware of the group size on your tour. Smaller groups may allow for more personalized interactions with the guide.

Post-Tour Exploration: After the tour, explore the sites you found most intriguing or revisit specific locations. You may discover more hidden gems.

Educational Experience: Treat the tour as an educational experience, where you not only learn about historical events but also gain a deeper appreciation for the city's evolution.

Some popular historic walking tours in St. Petersburg include those that explore downtown St. Petersburg, the waterfront, historic neighborhoods, and architectural highlights. Whether you're a history buff or simply interested in learning more about the city you're visiting, a walking tour offers an engaging and informative way to explore St. Petersburg's past and present.

106.Attend a live music event at a local venue.

St. Petersburg, Florida, has a lively music scene, with numerous local venues that host live music events featuring a wide range of musical genres. Whether you're into rock, jazz, blues, country, hip-hop, or indie music, you can find a local venue that suits your musical taste. Here's how to make the most of attending a live music event at a local venue in St. Petersburg:

Research Local Venues: Start by researching local music venues in St. Petersburg. Some popular venues include Jannus Live, The Palladium, The Ale and the Witch, The Hideaway, and Ruby's Elixir, among others. Check their event calendars for upcoming live music performances.

Genre Preferences: Determine your music genre preferences and look for venues that frequently host artists and bands in that genre. St. Petersburg's music scene caters to a diverse range of tastes.

Check the Schedule: Visit the venue's website or social media pages to check their schedule. Pay attention to the date and time of the live music event, as well as the featured artists or bands.

Purchase Tickets: If the event requires tickets, buy them in advance. Some venues offer online ticket sales, while others may have box offices where you can purchase tickets in person.

Arrive Early: Plan to arrive at the venue early, especially if you want to secure a good spot close to the stage. Early arrival also allows you to explore the venue and enjoy any pre-show entertainment or opening acts.

Dress Appropriately: Dress comfortably and appropriately for the venue and music style. Some venues have specific dress codes, so it's a good idea to check in advance.

Support Local Acts: St. Petersburg has a thriving local music scene, and you may find talented local bands and artists performing at smaller venues or open mic nights. Support local talent by attending their shows.

Enjoy the Atmosphere: Live music events offer more than just the music. Immerse yourself in the atmosphere, connect with fellow music enthusiasts, and savor the energy of a live performance.

Respect the Venue Rules: Follow the venue's rules and guidelines, including any age restrictions, alcohol policies, and security measures. Be courteous to fellow attendees and venue staff.

Discover New Music: Live music events are an excellent opportunity to discover new music. Be open to listening to artists you may not be familiar with – you might just find a new favorite.

Merchandise and Autographs: Some artists and bands sell merchandise like CDs, vinyl records, T-shirts, and posters at live shows. It's a chance to support the artists directly and even get an autograph.

Safety and Comfort: Ensure your own safety and comfort during the event. Stay hydrated, and protect your hearing by using earplugs if the music is very loud.

Attending a live music event at a local venue in St. Petersburg is a memorable and immersive experience. Whether you're there to see a well-known national act or to discover the city's local talent, it's an opportunity to enjoy music, connect with others, and create lasting memories.

107. Visit a local farmers' market.

Visiting a local farmers' market in St. Petersburg, Florida, is a delightful way to experience the city's vibrant community, sample fresh produce, and support local growers and artisans. Farmers' markets offer a variety of products, from locally sourced fruits and vegetables to artisanal goods and handmade crafts. Here's how to make the most of your visit to a farmers' market in St. Petersburg:

Research Markets: St. Petersburg has several farmers' markets that operate on different days and in various locations. Research the options and choose a market that fits your schedule and interests.

Market Hours: Farmers' markets typically have specific hours of operation. Check the market's schedule to ensure you arrive at a convenient time.

Bring Reusable Bags: Come prepared with reusable shopping bags or baskets to carry your purchases. This is eco-friendly and practical for transporting your goods.

Cash and Cards: While many vendors accept credit cards, it's a good idea to carry some cash in smaller denominations. Some vendors may only accept cash payments.

Stroll and Explore: Take your time to stroll through the market and explore the various stalls. You'll find fresh produce, locally made food items, artisanal goods, handcrafted items, and more.

Sample and Taste: Many vendors offer samples of their products, so don't hesitate to try new flavors and discover local specialties.

Local Produce: Look for seasonal and locally grown fruits and vegetables. These are often fresher and more flavorful than what you find in grocery stores.

Artisanal Products: Farmers' markets are a great place to find unique, handmade products such as jams, sauces, baked goods, cheeses, and honey.

Support Local Artisans: Many markets feature local artists and crafters. Consider purchasing handmade jewelry, pottery, artwork, and other crafts to support local talent.

Food Trucks: Some farmers' markets have food trucks or stalls offering ready-to-eat meals. This is an excellent opportunity to savor local flavors.

Live Entertainment: Some markets feature live music, entertainment, or even cooking demonstrations. Enjoy the lively atmosphere and community spirit.

Community Engagement: Interact with the vendors and learn more about their products and their commitment to sustainability and local agriculture.

Check Market Specials: Be on the lookout for special deals or discounts offered by vendors, especially toward the end of the market.

Bring the Family: Farmers' markets are often family-friendly, with activities for kids, pet-friendly policies, and a great atmosphere for all ages.

Plan Your Visit: Plan your visit around any specific items you're looking for or events happening at the market. Check the market's website or social media pages for updates.

Visiting a farmers' market in St. Petersburg provides an authentic and enjoyable way to connect with the local community, savor fresh and locally sourced products, and discover the creativity of local artisans. It's a perfect addition to your itinerary for a taste of St. Petersburg's culture and flavor.

108.Go thrift shopping in the city's thrift stores.

Thrift shopping in St. Petersburg, Florida, is a rewarding and eco-friendly way to explore the city's unique culture and find hidden treasures at affordable prices. Whether you're looking for vintage clothing, furniture, collectibles, or one-of-a-kind items, St. Petersburg's thrift stores have a lot to offer. Here's how to make the most of your thrift shopping adventure in the city:

Travel to St. Petersburg Florida

Research Thrift Stores: Begin by researching thrift stores in St. Petersburg. Some well-known options include the St. Vincent de Paul Thrift Store, Goodwill, and smaller independent shops. Each store may have its own specialty, so consider your interests when choosing where to go.

Store Hours: Check the store hours in advance, as they may vary by location. Some thrift stores open early, while others close late, so plan your visit accordingly.

Bring Cash: While many thrift stores now accept credit and debit cards, it's a good idea to carry some cash, especially for smaller purchases. Some stores may offer cash-only deals.

Dress Comfortably: Wear comfortable clothing and shoes that are easy to change in and out of if you plan to try on clothing. Avoid wearing complicated outfits or a lot of jewelry.

Inspect Items: Thoroughly inspect items before purchasing. Look for any flaws, wear, or damage, and ensure that clothing and accessories are clean and in good condition.

Dig Deep: Thrift stores often have a variety of items tucked away. Take your time to explore all sections, including clothing, furniture, electronics, books, and collectibles. You might find unique items in unexpected places.

Check for Discounts: Ask store staff if there are any special deals or discounts available on the day of your visit. Many thrift stores have regular sale days.

Haggle Politely: Some thrift stores are open to negotiation, especially if you're purchasing multiple items. Politely ask if they can offer a discount, and be prepared to pay the listed price if they decline.

Bring a Reusable Bag: Bring a reusable shopping bag to carry your purchases. This is not only eco-friendly but also convenient for transporting your finds.

Support Local Stores: Consider visiting locally owned and operated thrift stores. These stores often have a unique selection of items and provide a more personalized shopping experience.

Ask for Recommendations: If you're looking for something specific, don't hesitate to ask store staff for recommendations. They might have insights into where to find particular items in the store.

Be Patient: Thrift shopping can require patience. You may not find what you're looking for on your first visit, so enjoy the thrill of the hunt and visit different stores periodically.

Thrift shopping in St. Petersburg offers a chance to discover vintage fashion, retro home decor, and an array of eclectic items that you won't find in mainstream retail stores. It's an eco-conscious and budget-friendly way to explore the city's unique character and uncover some hidden gems.

109.Join a community gardening project.

Joining a community gardening project in St. Petersburg, Florida, is a rewarding way to connect with the local community, contribute to sustainable agriculture, and enjoy the outdoors. Community gardens offer the opportunity to grow your own produce, learn about gardening, and make new friends who share similar interests. Here's how to get started with a community gardening project:

Research Local Community Gardens: Begin by researching community gardens in St. Petersburg. There are often several options to choose from, each with its own unique atmosphere and focus. Look for gardens that are conveniently located for you.

Visit the Garden: Once you've identified a garden of interest, visit it to get a feel for the space, meet some of the gardeners, and learn about the garden's specific requirements and guidelines. Many gardens have open houses or regular workdays that you can attend.

Contact the Garden Organizer: Reach out to the garden organizer or coordinator to express your interest in joining. They can provide you with information on membership, plot availability, and any fees associated with participation.

Understand the Commitment: Be sure you understand the commitment involved. Community gardens often require members to attend workdays, maintain their individual plots, and follow specific guidelines. Ask about any time or work requirements.

Prepare for Gardening: Acquire the necessary gardening tools, seeds or plants, and soil amendments to get started. Some community gardens may provide tools or resources for their members.

Learn and Share: Engage with fellow gardeners to learn from their experiences and share your own knowledge. Community gardens are excellent places for exchanging gardening tips and advice.

Respect the Rules: Follow the rules and guidelines set by the community garden. These rules may include guidelines on organic gardening, composting, and what can be grown in your plot.

Participate in Garden Activities: Get involved in garden activities and social events. Many community gardens organize workshops, potlucks, and community workdays that help build a sense of camaraderie among members.

Harvest and Share: Enjoy the fruits of your labor by harvesting your own produce. Community gardens often allow you to keep what you grow, but consider sharing your surplus with fellow gardeners or donating to local charities.

Be Environmentally Conscious: Practice sustainable gardening by using natural and eco-friendly methods to nurture your plants. Composting and responsible water usage are essential.

Document Your Progress: Keep a gardening journal or take photos to document your gardening journey. This can help you learn from your experiences and track your progress over time.

Community gardening projects not only provide the opportunity to cultivate fresh, healthy food but also foster a sense of belonging and environmental responsibility. It's a wonderful way to engage with nature, meet like-minded individuals, and make a positive impact in your local community.

110.Take a scenic drive through local parks.

Taking a scenic drive through local parks in St. Petersburg, Florida, is a wonderful way to appreciate the city's natural beauty and lush green spaces. The city offers various parks and scenic routes that are perfect for a leisurely drive. Here are some parks and routes to explore:

Boyd Hill Nature Preserve: Enjoy a leisurely drive through Boyd Hill Nature Preserve, where you can admire the diverse ecosystems, including pine flatwoods and wetlands. Keep an eye out for wildlife and enjoy the tranquility of this natural oasis.

Fort De Soto Park: Fort De Soto Park is a beautiful coastal park with scenic drives along the shore. Explore the park's various beaches, watch for seabirds, and take in the stunning views of the Gulf of Mexico.

Weedon Island Preserve: Drive through Weedon Island Preserve and take in the serene landscapes of mangroves, waterways, and tidal flats. The preserve offers opportunities for birdwatching and scenic overlooks.

Sawgrass Lake Park: This park features a scenic boardwalk surrounded by a freshwater lake and a unique sawgrass prairie. It's a great place for a relaxing drive with opportunities for bird and wildlife watching.

Sunken Gardens: While Sunken Gardens is primarily a place to walk and explore on foot, the area surrounding it offers charming streets and neighborhoods for a scenic drive. The gardens themselves are a beautiful stop for a stroll.

Largo Central Park: Largo Central Park is a family-friendly park with lovely grounds for a peaceful drive. Enjoy the scenery, have a picnic, or take a walk around the park's beautiful lake.

Lake Seminole Park: Drive along the roads surrounding Lake Seminole Park and appreciate the scenic views of the lake and its surroundings. The park also offers recreational activities and walking trails.

Philippe Park: Located in nearby Safety Harbor, Philippe Park is a historic park with scenic drives under the shade of majestic oak trees. Take a relaxing drive through the park and learn about its history.

Fred Marquis Pinellas Trail: This multi-use trail extends for nearly 40 miles and passes through several parks and communities in Pinellas County, including St. Petersburg. Drive along parts of the trail for a scenic journey through the area.

City Streets and Waterfront Drives: St. Petersburg's downtown area and waterfront provide beautiful cityscape and water views. Cruise along the waterfront and through the city's charming streets to take in the urban scenery.

Travel to St. Petersburg Florida

Before embarking on your scenic drive, check for park hours, road conditions, and any entry fees that may apply. Whether you're interested in coastal views, lush landscapes, or urban scenery, a scenic drive through local parks in St. Petersburg allows you to enjoy the natural and cultural beauty of the area at your own pace.

Conclusion

St. Petersburg, Florida, offers a rich tapestry of history that has profoundly shaped the city's identity, character, and growth. From its modest beginnings as a small fishing village in the late 19th century, St. Petersburg has experienced a remarkable journey of transformation, evolution, and innovation.

Its transformation from a sleepy village into a burgeoning resort town was catalyzed by the arrival of the Orange Belt Railway and the vision of early pioneers like Peter Demens, who laid the foundations for the city's growth. St. Petersburg's reputation as a winter retreat for the wealthy elite began to take shape, with the establishment of luxury hotels and the development of recreational activities such as golf and tennis.

During the early 20th century, the city became an epicenter of aviation history as pioneers like Tony Jannus flew the world's first scheduled airline service across Tampa Bay. This historic flight was a testament to the city's spirit of innovation and adventure.

The mid-20th century brought both prosperity and challenges, as the city expanded and experienced economic growth. However, St. Petersburg also played a significant role in the Civil Rights Movement, with residents and leaders working tirelessly to combat racial segregation and discrimination.

In recent decades, St. Petersburg has embraced a new chapter in its history, focusing on sustainability, cultural enrichment, and economic diversification. The city's commitment to environmental conservation, including its thriving waterfront parks and initiatives to combat climate change, underscores its forward-thinking approach.

Today, St. Petersburg stands as a vibrant, diverse, and inclusive city with a thriving economy, a flourishing arts scene, and a strong sense of community. Its well-preserved historic districts, cultural institutions, beautiful parks, and pristine beaches continue to be cherished by residents and visitors alike.

As St. Petersburg looks to the future, it does so with a deep appreciation for its past. The city's history is not just a collection of facts and events; it is a living narrative that informs its culture, values, and aspirations. St. Petersburg remains a place where history, culture, and progress intersect, making it a captivating destination and an inspiring community for all who have the pleasure of experiencing it.

Travel to St. Petersburg Florida

If you enjoyed, please leave a 5-star Amazon Review

To get a free list of people who knows publishing top places to travel all around the world, click this link
https://bit.ly/peoplewhoknowtravel

References

Rcsprinter123, CC BY-SA 3.0 <https://creativecommons.org/licenses/by-sa/3.0>, via Wikimedia Commons
https://pixabay.com/photos/strawberry-dessert-strawberries-2191973/

Made in the USA
Columbia, SC
02 July 2025

60237163R00104